CHICKEN SOUP FOR THE SOUL® LOVE STORIES

CHICKEN SOUP FOR THE SOUL® LOVE STORIES

Jack Canfield
Mark Victor Hansen
and Peter Vegso

Health Communications, Inc.
Deerfield Beach, Florida

www.hcibooks.com
www.chickensoup.com

We would like to acknowledge the many publishers and individuals who granted us permission to reprint the cited material.

Turtledoves. Reprinted by Erin McCarty © 2002 Erin McCarty.

Finding Love Where You Least Expect It. Reprinted by permission of Sarah R. Smiley. © 2005 Sarah R. Smiley.

A Change of Plans. Reprinted by permission of Carol Bryant. © 2002 Carol Bryant.

Taking the Time. Reprinted by permission of Samantha Waltz. © 2007 Samantha Waltz.

(Continued on page 285)

Library of Congress Cataloging-in-Publication Data

Chicken soup for the soul love stories : stories of first dates, soul mates, and everlasting love / Jack Canfield . . . [et al.].
    p. cm.
    Includes bibliographical references.
    ISBN-13: 978-0-7573-0663-1 (trade paper)
    ISBN-10: 0-7573-0663-2 (trade paper)
    1. Man–woman relationships. 2. Love stories, American.
I. Canfield, Jack, 1944–
HQ801.C4785 2008
306.7—dc22

               2007037728

    Scripture quotation marked NIV taken from the *Holy Bible, New International Version®. NIV®.* Copyright © 1973, 1978, 1984 International Bible Society. Used by permission of Zondervan. All rights reserved.
    Scripture quotations marked NKJV are taken from the New King James Version. Copyright © 1982 by Thomas Nelson, Inc. Used by permission. All rights reserved.

Publisher: Health Communications, Inc.
          3201 S.W. 15th Street
          Deerfield Beach, FL 33442-8190

Cover design by Andrea Perrine Brower
Inside formatting by Dawn Von Strolley Grove

Contents

3. GRATITUDE

4. OVERCOMING OBSTACLES

5. THROUGH THE EYES OF A CHILD

6. INSIGHTS AND LESSONS

Acknowledgments

We wish to express our heartfelt gratitude to all of the people who helped make this book possible:

Our families, who have been chicken soup for our souls by supporting us as we continue to serve our readers endlessly!

Russ Kamalski, the most amazing chief operating officer on the planet, who can take any situation and make it simple.

D'ette Corona and Barbara LoMonaco, who seamlessly manage twenty to thirty projects at a time. Without them none of these projects would happen.

Patty Hansen, our president of the legal and licensing division. Patty is magnificent at the day-to-day challenges.

Veronica Romero, Lisa Williams, Teresa Collett, Robin Yerian, Jesse Ianniello, Lauren Edelstein, Lauren Bray, Debbie Lefever, Connie Simoni, Karen Schoenfeld, Marty Robinson, Patti Coffey, Pat Burns, Kristi Waite, and Blake Arce who support Jack's and Mark's businesses with skill and love.

Laurie Hartman and Patti Clement, who support our Costa Mesa operation with skill and love.

Michele Matrisciani, Carol Rosenberg, Andrea Gold, Allison Janse, and Katheline St. Fort, our editors at Health Communications, Inc., for their devotion to excellence.

Lori Golden, Kelly Maragni, Sean Geary, Patricia McConnell, Kim Weiss, and Paola Fernandez-Rana, for doing such an incredible job supporting our books.

Tom Sand, Claude Choquette, and Luc Jutras, who manage year after year to get our books translated into more than forty languages around the world.

The Art Department at Health Communications, Inc., for their talent, creativity, and unrelenting patience in producing book covers and inside designs that capture the essence of Chicken Soup: Larissa Hise Henoch, Lawna Patterson Oldfield, Andrea Perrine Brower, Anthony Clausi, Peter Quintal, and Dawn Von Strolley Grove.

Patricia Brady, for editing the final manuscript with such enthusiasm. Your willingness to help and your friendship means the world to all of us.

And, most of all, thanks to everyone who submitted their heartfelt stories, poems, quotes, and cartoons for possible inclusion in this book. While we were not able to use everything you sent in, we know that each word came from a magical place flourishing within your soul.

Because of the size of this project, we may have left out the names of some people who contributed along the way. If so, we are sorry, but please know that we really do appreciate you very much. We are truly grateful and love you all!

Introduction

One day while in seventh grade, as you open your locker, you see a small snowflakelike note peeping out of the gray vents. Curious, you snatch the note, then race to third-period study hall to see what this mysterious little slip of paper contains.

As you fall into your desk chair, the snowflake drops onto your lap. Excited, you look down and see *your name* precisely written on the small flap. Once your hands stop shaking, you open the note and find *you have a secret admirer!*

Now every day at the end of each class, you swing by your locker to check to see if any more special notes have been delivered. But after one week the school year is over, and no more snowflakes arrive.

For the first two of the three summer months, you mope and talk to anyone who will listen to your cruel twist of fate. But then the neighbor's thirteen-year-old cousin arrives for a two-week vacation and you are smitten. You conveniently dismiss the anonymous note as stupid kid stuff.

"That's the power of love," sings Huey Lewis.

That same power carries through to all ages (as our coauthors faithfully wrote), but love takes on a mystique that is sometimes hard to decode. Children are certain their parents, who seem so old and never show signs of romance, could not possibly love each other. They do not see love in the gentle subtleties of a romantic glance or when parents cheer wildly at their not-so-successful piano recital. But when old enough, these same children will take a stray cat into their homes, call a friend who just lost a job, and yes, cheer wildly at a loved one's basketball game.

A word for the hardnosed personalities of the world who continue to look at love as a weakness or frailty: the most admired individuals show love and devotion to the people they serve. It's no surprise when asked, "Whom did you admire the most in your lifetime?" that the top vote usually goes to a parent, teacher, or friend who showed love through work, discipline, kindness, and caring.

Yes—that's the power of love.

Share with Us

We would love to hear your reactions to the stories in this book. Please let us know what your favorite stories were and how they affected you.

We also invite you to send us stories you would like to see published in future editions of Chicken Soup for the Soul. Please send submissions to: www.chickensoup.com.

Chicken Soup for the Soul
P.O. Box 30880
Santa Barbara, CA 93130
fax: 805-563-2945

We hope you enjoy reading this book as much as we enjoyed compiling and editing it.

Turtledoves

They walk along together,
A couple holding hands
And never caring whether
The sight of them demands
Responses less than seemly:
A point, a laugh, a stare.
Her hazel eyes are dreamy;
He loses himself there.
Time melts away, revealing
A boy and girl in love.
With poplars for a ceiling,
Heralded by doves,
They stroll the cobbled pathway,
A golden life ahead.
The vision fades. It's today,
And standing there instead,
Forever by his side,
Is the woman he adores.
He cherishes his bride
More deeply than before
In spite of all the creases,
The creaks and silver strands.
He knows nothing but peace as
They wander, holding hands.

Erin McCarty

1

HOW WE MET

I am falling like a falling star who has finally found her place next to another in a lovely constellation, where we will sparkle in the heavens together.

Amy Tan

Finding Love Where You Least Expect It

Any emotion, if it is sincere, is involuntary.

Mark Twain

"I can't believe you're making me do this," I yelled downstairs to my mom as I hopped on one foot from my bedroom to the bathroom, trying to fasten a sandal.

"Just go and have fun," my mom called back. "It's not like you have to marry him."

Two weeks before, my mom had been in contact with a long-lost family friend. Our families had been neighbors until I was in the fifth grade. Coincidentally, they had a son who was one year older than I was.

In the course of catching up on the past ten years, my mom and his mom had arranged a date between the boy and me. (Although, at the age of twenty-one, he could hardly be called a "boy" anymore, but that's the way I remembered him.)

I hurriedly dressed and brushed my hair (a little haphazardly, with low enthusiasm for my date), and I thought about the boy I used to know.

I remembered being told that when he was only one year old, he brought a baby gift to my mom the day I was born. I thought of an old photograph in my scrapbook, his arm around me as we waited to go inside church for Easter service. As an awkward ten-year-old, I hid behind my mom when he tried to talk to me.

I remembered him as a self-conscious twelve-year-old, with buckteeth and a round belly. We went to the same elementary school, and when we passed in the hall, I would lower my head and avoid eye contact, trying desperately not to be noticed. But he always spotted me and managed to embarrass himself with an awkward "hello."

What have I gotten myself into? I thought as I quickly coated my lashes with mascara and gave one final glance at myself in the mirror.

The doorbell rang. I heard my mom walk to the front door. I stood silent, listening.

"Well, hello!" My mom was full of hospitality and enthusiasm. "It is so great to see you after all this time."

He answered back with an uncomfortable and embarrassed voice. I rolled my eyes.

This is going to be loads of fun, I thought sarcastically.

The phone rang. It was my best friend calling to see if I had met "my date" yet.

"No," I said, "but I hear him talking to my mom downstairs, and he sounds really dorky."

Then I had an idea: "Hey, why don't you meet us tonight? That way, if things don't go well, I'll have an excuse to leave and end the date."

My friend was game, more out of curiosity than a willingness to help me, so we arranged to meet at a restaurant downtown.

I walked down the stairs, trying to plan a last-minute escape. Could I feign illness? Fall and break my leg? Run out the front door and hide until he finally left?

I followed my mom's voice coming from the kitchen and reluctantly walked toward the noise, dragging my feet as if I wore cement shoes.

As I turned the corner and entered the kitchen, I saw him immediately.

Has there been some mistake? I thought. He didn't look like the boy I remembered.

He was sitting at the kitchen table, across from my mom. He had impeccable posture, with broad, muscular shoulders. His face was tanned. His hair was dark and perfectly trimmed. His deep brown eyes glistened as he smiled at me. And his teeth—his glorious teeth—were perfectly straight (years of braces, I thought) and brilliantly white.

"Hi," he said. "It's nice to see you again."

His face was beaming. A strange, unexpected electricity filled the air.

He stood to shake my hand. He was tall and fit, and well-dressed, too. He was confident and poised—so different from the shy boy I was expecting.

I was speechless. I stuttered and stammered a feeble "hello" before shaking his strong hand.

Nervously I said, "Uh, I think I forgot something." I ran back up the stairs and shut myself in the bathroom.

My heart was racing. That was no boy in the kitchen—certainly not the awkward boy I remembered. He was a man—a very handsome, polite man.

Adrenaline filled my ears and made them burn. My hands were shaking. I threw open drawers and began redoing my makeup—this time with care and precision. I brushed my hair and straightened my dress.

Should I change clothes? I wondered. *No, that would be too obvious, too weird.*

I walked back downstairs, giddy with nerves and excitement. We said good-bye to my mom, and he put his hand at the small of my back to lead me to his car. I was shaking.

As we sat side by side in the car, I discovered his charm went far beyond the handsome smile and strong physique. Our conversation became effortless, with no stops or awkward gaps. We told stories from our childhood and laughed about the times we had been so nervous around each other. We learned we had a great deal in common, that our connection was deeper than the history we shared.

My friend met us at the restaurant, ready to save me from my blind date. But she wasn't needed.

"You can go home," I told her. "Things are great; I'm having fun."

"Are you sure?" she asked. "You hardly know this guy."

"Actually, I've known him all my life," I said. "And I think I'm going to marry him one day."

Two years later, I did marry him. And one year after that, we had our own little boy.

In our den, next to wedding photos and a picture of our son's first birthday, a photograph of two children—one three years old and the other four—hangs above the couch in an antique brass frame. The boy has his arm around the girl. They are sitting outside a church—he in his Easter suit and she in her new dress and bonnet. The girl is shy and looking at the ground. The boy has a twinkle in his eye. He is smiling at the camera, smiling at me as I walk past the picture on the wall.

Could it be, I often wonder, *that the boy knew all along?*

Sarah Smiley

"I don't remember you being a
hunka hunka hottie hoo-rah when we were kids."

A Change of Plans

I was a twenty-eight-year-old nurse in need of a change. My life was in turmoil, and the chance to work as a traveling nurse in Hawaii seemed to be an ideal opportunity. My plan was to work for four months, while exploring the islands in my free time. I would sit alone on the beach, ponder my future, and then return to New York to resume my life in the big city.

Meanwhile, on the other side of the world, a young man was also in need of a change. Accounting in his hometown of Sydney had left him restless. His new plan was to work as a flight attendant for two or three years, see the world, and then resume his well-ordered life in Australia.

That day in August was like most days on Oahu: sunny and warm with palm trees swaying in the breeze. I planned to bike over Diamond Head to Hanauma Bay and join friends for a day at the beach. I envisioned a day lazing in the shade with a good book. I was down on men but high on Hawaii.

When I reached Hanauma Bay, I faced a dilemma. I wanted to lock my bike with my friends' bikes, but I had forgotten the combination. The bike racks were in the parking lot on a cliff high above the beach. I needed to leave my bike with someone I could trust while I searched for my friends on the beach far below.

That's when I noticed a sweaty, red-faced young man sitting in the shade of a banyan tree. Judging from his flushed face and his bicycle propped against the tree, I assumed that he planned to sit in the shade a bit longer. He wasn't much to look at, with his damp hair plastered to his forehead, but he seemed safe enough. And since he already had a bike, I doubted he would steal mine.

He agreed to watch my bike while I hiked down the hill to find my friends. When I finally returned and secured my bike in the rack, he asked if he could join my group. I wasn't thrilled with the prospect of giving up my solitude to keeping company with a stranger, but I couldn't really refuse since he had been guarding my bike for the past twenty minutes.

Then he asked if I'd go snorkeling with him. *Snorkeling? What a pest!* Visions of reading in that quiet spot in the shade seemed to grow even dimmer. I told him that I didn't have any money to rent equipment. He offered to pay. What was I to do?

As the day wore on and the beach started to empty, I learned that his name was Phil, that he, too, was twenty-eight, and that this was his first time in the States. His accent was a bit hard to follow, and we had to resort to spelling words at times to communicate. He was the first Australian I had ever met, and I was amazed at the differences in our common language.

Although I still wasn't excited about making small talk with someone I didn't know, I discovered that Phil was easy to talk to. And he had been very sweet to watch my bike and to pay for my snorkeling equipment. Before I knew it, I heard myself offering to buy him a beer for his generosity. I had arranged to meet him at his hotel for one beer, just one, before joining my friends for the evening.

A few hours later in the hotel lobby, I spotted one of the best looking men I had seen for a long time walking toward me. Tall and dark, Phil was a cross between Tom Sellick and Burt Reynolds. *He certainly scrubs up well,* I thought. I later learned that those were his exact thoughts about me. Apparently, I hadn't been much to look at after cycling over Diamond Head either.

We spent the evening dancing in the disco at the top of his hotel. It offered a panoramic view of Waikiki, with mountain silhouettes to the west and the lights of the marina to the east.

The next few days we spent discovering just how romantic Hawaii is. We caught the bus to a beach popular with the locals for body surfing. We hiked to Sacred Falls and swam in the icy pool at the foot of the falls. We watched fabulous sunsets from the patio of his hotel while sipping exotic drinks. The air smelled sweet, tropical flowers bloomed on every corner, and we seemed to be surrounded by couples in love.

It was an extraordinary few days, made all the more special by the knowledge that it was only temporary. Phil would return to Sydney, and our time together would be just memories. I felt safe knowing that he would be half a world away. I had no plans to become involved with anyone at this point in my life.

But plans changed. Phil managed to swap schedules with his good mate Nyle and surprised me with a visit in October. We spent the time on Kauai. We swam at a secluded beach on the Na Pali coast, which could only be reached by hiking through a tropical rain forest. We took a Zodiac raft trip even farther along the rugged coast, through caves, to view a part of the island accessible only to boats and serious hikers. We spent the last night in a rustic cabin in the national park surrounding Waimea Canyon. Kauai lacked the nightlife of Waikiki but offered more remote beaches for long walks in the moonlight. This time when we said good-bye, we planned to meet in New York after my nursing assignment finished, so that I could show Phil another side of the States.

Once again, plans changed. In December Phil returned for my last week in Hawaii. It was our chance to explore Maui. We hiked into Haleakala Crater, ate ice cream cones with the tourists in Lahaina, and drove the dizzying road to Seven Sacred Pools. We raised the rite of picnicking to new heights with champagne toasts on cliffs overlooking the pounding winter surf of the Pacific.

Perhaps it was when we were standing on the rim of Haleakala Crater, wrapped together in a blanket, watching the sunrise; or while we hiked through the bamboo forest to Jackass Ginger Falls, the air heavy with the scent of ginger and plumeria; or when we ate a midnight snack of tempura mahi-mahi sandwiches in a diner on Hotel Street. At some point, before I was ready to admit it to myself, our plans for the rest of our lives changed.

Now—twenty-five years, two kids, and one mortgage later—our plans are to someday return to visit the places where we each took a chance and opened our hearts to a stranger. The kids plan to join us, too. That's one plan we definitely plan to keep.

Carol Bryant

Taking the Time

All love that has not friendship for its base, is like a mansion built upon the sand.

Ella Wheeler Wilcox

I spotted Ray immediately. He stood out as the most handsome man in a group of thirty singles sipping wine and subtly checking one another out. Divorced seven years, I had fine-tuned my ability to spot a good-looking man without a gold ring on his left hand.

About the same time, Ray's eyes swept around the hotel lounge and caught my gaze. He smiled—a terrific, crooked smile—and took a few steps toward me.

Another woman, dressed in basic black with a stunning jade necklace, who obviously took an interest in Ray, stepped between us and started chatting with him. I heard words like "golf" and "eighty-two" and "that seventh hole." Apparently they had already met on the golf course, perhaps at an event, like this theater evening, sponsored by the activities club to which I belonged. I turned to talk with a man to my right, hoping my quick smile covered my disappointment.

The woman who planned the evening handed me a ticket to the play. "I put you by that guy over there," she whispered, nodding in Ray's direction. "He's new to the club. I figured you'd make him comfortable."

So, I would get to meet him after all.

Eventually Ray and I wound up side by side at a table of hors d'oeuvres, spreading brie on crackers. We talked about the kind of inane topics one discusses at events like this: the weather, our jobs, an upcoming hike sponsored by the club. Ray compared his ticket to mine and noted that we were seated next to each other.

He had dressed well for the evening: gray slacks and a navy blazer. I could tell he would look equally good in shorts and a polo shirt out on the golf course.

That evening promised to be memorable for me. But Ray talked of nothing except his work as we walked the half mile from the hotel to the theater. I had little interest in the woes of a restaurant owner. I went home thinking about the play we'd seen, not Ray.

I doubt he gave me a second thought, either. I had a cold and had coughed or sucked on cough drops throughout the performance. At intermission, when Ray and I might have been sharing refreshments, I went outside and hacked into the warm summer air.

It was not love at first sight.

Several weeks later I went with a male buddy to a dance for singles cosponsored by three singles clubs. A small local band filled the air with a rhythm that set my foot tapping. Magic touched my dance shoes as I waltzed and foxtrotted, cha-cha'd and rumba'd with a number of different men for at least an hour.

When the band took a break, my last dance partner and I sat down to catch our breath. Soon he went to get us drinks.

Then Ray approached, flashing that terrific smile. He drew a chair up to the table, and we chatted for a few minutes. Had I thought any more about the play we had seen together? Did he think the clouds gathering outside threatened an early summer storm? Wasn't the band outstanding? Ray seemed more at ease than he had the night of the play—funnier and more interesting. I was eager to dance with him. But when the band took the stage again and the music started, he just kept talking. I dropped hints about the beat of the song. He talked some more. I finally asked him to dance.

Ray's sense of rhythm wasn't as great as his smile. He mumbled something about how I had obviously taken a lot more dance lessons than he had, and then we finished the song in an uneasy silence. As another number started up, we thanked each other for the dance we had shared and wandered in separate directions to find new partners.

It wasn't love at second sight, either.

A week later, exhausted from several hectic days of administering final exams to my high school students, I wanted to crawl into bed with a good book. But a girlfriend called and asked me to go to another singles' dance. The last thing I wanted was to push myself to get dressed up and act clever, friendly, and upbeat, but she talked me into going. Then when I had my face, hair, and evening bag ready, she called to say that she had decided to stay home. Since I was overdressed for crawling into bed with a book, I picked up the car keys and headed out.

When I walked into the ballroom, a bit nervous about going alone, I promptly saw several men I knew. Relieved, I found an empty chair along a wall and put on my dance shoes. There was no live band; Instead a DJ played nonstop music, mostly swing. Like the week before, I danced till I was breathless.

I headed toward the ladies' room to freshen my lipstick,

when I saw Ray enter the room with a small group of people I didn't know. I judged from their dress that they had come to the dance after a round of Friday night golf. Ray wore a yellow polo shirt that showed off a nice tan as well as an appealing set of biceps—and again, that fabulous smile.

My knees grew weak. Maybe we had parted ways too hastily after that first dance.

"Hi," I said. "Nice to see you again."

He returned a greeting that was just as welcoming. We visited for a bit, and then he pulled me in to dance. We danced closer than I would have wanted to if his arms hadn't felt so comfortable. He put his cheek against mine, and I leaned into him, as we swayed in time to the music.

After several songs he led me to the table where his friends had gathered and introduced me all around. A man I knew approached, obviously intending to ask me to dance. "I'm going on the club hike to Tunnel Falls in the morning," Ray said before the man swept me onto the dance floor.

"I could do that," I said over my shoulder. Not that Ray had actually asked me to join him, but I wanted to see him again. I was starting to notice something about him besides his looks: a sweetness and gentleness.

I woke the next morning excited. I could take on a thirteen-mile hike, no sweat—well, maybe some sweat, since I hadn't hiked in a while. Then I heard the rain peppering my bedroom window. When I pulled aside the curtains I saw a deluge. Gathering all the confidence I'd been working on since my divorce, I pulled out my club directory and called Ray. "It's pouring. Do you want to go to breakfast instead of hiking?" I asked.

"You aren't afraid of a little rain, are you?" he answered.

A challenge? Now he really had my attention. I mentally inventoried my rain gear and said I'd meet him at the trailhead.

Club hikes usually draw twenty or more participants. That morning only five showed up. But during the thirteen miles we hiked, something about Ray soaked in along with the rain. It might have been the way he took my cold hands in his, rubbing them to increase circulation and worrying that I might chill. And, yes, that smile helped. It might have been how much we had in common: We both had kids in college who were spending the summer at home; we both had elderly parents close by for whom we felt responsible; we were both on the same political and religious spectra; we both liked to do many of the same things.

We talked nonstop about our interests, our families, our hopes, our fears. Sometimes Ray was funny, sometimes philosophical.

After the hike, we both cleared our calendars. Because we had each "been around the block," and over the big "5-0" hill as well, we had gotten off to a slow start. But we both wanted to switch gears and find out what was developing between us.

As Ray and I approach our eighth wedding anniversary, I am grateful I didn't let my first night's impression of him rule my heart. Or my second. For Ray and me, three meetings was definitely the charm.

Samantha Waltz

My Soul Mate

I saw him standing in the driveway as I drove past the house and didn't really think much of him. All the girls I knew thought he was the greatest. I just didn't see it. I guess I was at a point in my life where I was sick of dating and the games men played. My heart had just been broken, and I didn't want to have to deal with heartache again.

Rachel, my roommate, flew into our apartment excited a couple days later. She had talked to Travis, the guy all the girls were crazy about. I told her that was great and urged her to talk to him more and maybe ask him out. But Rachel was shy and didn't feel she could bring herself to do that.

A few days later Rachel talked me into going to a dance. She didn't want to go alone because Travis was going to be there. Anything to support a friend, I guess.

They seemed to get along okay. I still didn't see what was so great about this guy. At the end of the night, I saw the opportunity for Rachel to spend more time with him. I offered to drive Travis home with us. It was in the car that I discovered there was so much more to this guy than just good looks. He was hilarious! Travis made me laugh more than I ever remembered laughing in my entire life.

Rachel and I started spending more and more time with Travis and his friend Dave. Every time Rachel and I hung out with him, Rachel would clam up. I felt the awkwardness in the air, So I would make small talk with Travis. But the more we talked, the more we discovered we had in common—everyone around us seemed to disappear. I felt myself wanting to fall for him but wouldn't let myself. Rachel was my friend, and I couldn't hurt her like that.

At home one night, Rachel confronted me with my attraction to Travis. I desperately tried to deny my feelings, but apparently they were obvious to not only her, but also to others as well. She told me to pursue Travis. She wanted me to be happy because I had been so sad lately. Then she smiled and admitted that she was a lot more interested in his friend anyway.

I saw Travis the next day, and it felt different: it was like seeing him for the first time. We talked for hours. I guess Travis was just waiting for me to wake up and realize that it was me he was interested in.

Through our conversation that day, I found out he was from the same small town where my mother had been born and raised. I had spent just about every summer there while growing up. Travis thought it was great that we had been in the same town while we were kids but had never known it.

Excited, I called my mom when I got home to tell her all about Travis. She couldn't believe I had met someone from her hometown, since most people have not even heard of it, let alone been from there. When I told my mom his last name, she urged me to find out his dad's name. So the next day I asked Travis.

"Mom, his dad's name is Glen," I said.

All I could hear was giggling on the other end of the phone.

"Mom, what is so funny?"

"Well," she said, "I never told you about the boy who was my school crush. All through elementary and high school I liked this boy. His name was Glen."

"I don't even believe this, Mom! You are telling me that I am dating the son of the man that you liked all through school?"

"Oh, but there is more," my mom said. "I have kept contact with all my friends from back home. When you were little and we used to visit my hometown, we would get together with my old girlfriends and their kids. You played with Travis as a child." I could not even believe this. "Are you sure this is the right person that you are thinking of, Mom?"

"Michelle, I am positive."

I told Travis the next day. A big smile stretched across his face.

"I knew there was a reason I liked you so much, and now you have confirmed it for me."

We went to a dance a couple of nights later. Brian, the guy who had broken up with me just before I met Travis, was there. He was obviously jealous that I had shown up with a new guy. He competed for my attention all evening. I became very confused. I was attracted to Travis, and everything seemed to click with us. But then there was Brian, and he had been a friend for so long. He had broken my heart, and now he was giving me the attention I had always hoped for.

A slow song began, and Travis grabbed my hand and led me to the dance floor. As we danced he held me ever so gently. He smelled so good.

The song ended and he let me go. But then he reached out, pulled me back, and whispered in my ear, "That was my favorite part of tonight, and I would give anything to have more of those moments."

My heart melted, and at that moment I knew: Travis was the man God had intended for me—my soul mate, my true love.

Together for six years and wed for four, Travis and I are now blessed with two beautiful children.

I thank God every day for the life he has blessed me with. And I thank him for letting me live my dream with the man of my dreams—my soul mate.

Michelle Lawson

"Have fun, kids—try to play nice
like you did last time together . . . in preschool."

Romance Amid Turmoil

*Love would never be a promise of a rose garden
unless it is showered with a light of faith, water
of sincerity, and an art of passion.*

Source Unknown

World War II, in all its savagery and destruction, set my romantic and blissful future.

My infantry unit was in a rest area in Metz, France, in early 1945, after a long session on the active front with Patton's tank units. Relaxing on an overstuffed lounge, the freedom from tension and anxiety felt druglike and over-powering. After three years of intensive and nerve-racking abuse of mind and body, this was a new world. A mirage appeared, dreamlike before my open eyes: civilian life extraordinaire with its enviable luxuries—women, music, and entertainment. Life suddenly became worthwhile once again.

But short! The dream vanished like a haze in sunlight as reality poked its nose into my fantasies. My name was called several times before I was conscious enough to realize that the mail was being delivered.

Wow, a letter from my sister in the big city. Further, she mentioned a pretty nurse tending to her needs when she had recently given birth to a baby boy, and to whom my dear sibling endeavored to give three good reasons for corresponding with me. My sister gave her nurse my photo, and she also talked a lot about me.

The nurse's attitude was passive, and her promises to write me never resulted in any letters. However, my interest became unbelievably aroused, and I decided to take an aggressive approach. I wrote the initial epistle, the first link in a blind courtship.

Enchanted by her first reply and highly elated by her second, which contained her snapshot, I was entranced! She was gorgeous. Yes! This was it! Suddenly, I knew that this was the girl I would marry.

The thought sent shivers of delight up my spine. I considered myself a most fortunate young man.

A rose has its thorns. I realized that the distance that separated us was a great handicap. If I were to succeed in my ultimate purpose, I needed to plan my strategy wisely.

My hope hung on my success in pleasing and surprising her, which was quite difficult to accomplish long distance. In addition to conducting a yearlong prosaic letter-writing courtship, I showered her with a varied assortment of delightful trinkets, perfumes, and historically valuable items. For her birthday, I wired her a beautiful orchid, an act which I later discovered gained me an ally—her mother. Oh, happy day!

At long last my military duties ended, and it was off to the States. The trip was exceedingly long, my patience almost exhausted. My blood pressure was above normal, my anxieties overwhelming.

I had seen only pictures of her, but the waiting would soon end, and I would see her face-to-face. Nevertheless, devilish thoughts persisted and threatened to suffocate me. The suspense was unbearable: *Are the pictures I carry really of her? Was she exaggerating in her intriguing letters?* Time was endless!

At last, I was a civilian! Fantastic! The albatross disappeared. I felt lighter. With great anticipation, I set out a day later on a mission more exciting and exhilarating than anything I had ever known. I hoped for the best—for a happy future.

I left New York City for Utica, New York, where she was a cadet nurse lieutenant in Rhoad's General Hospital. The five-hour train trip was an eternity. Finally I saw a glitter of the rainbow. I phoned her, and I could feel the throbbing excitement in her voice also. I was to meet her that evening in my hotel lobby.

I took a deep breath and tried to steady myself. *Okay! That is better.* I walked into the lobby, my eyes searching for the dream.

A nurse waved to me.

Ah! But no! It couldn't be. She knew me, but she wasn't the one.

Shocking realization that I was tricked sent trickles of sweat down my forehead. My disappointment must have been evident to the waving nurse, for she smiled quickly and motioned to another seated behind her, who immediately arose.

Fate treated me well at last. My relief knew no bounds. I treaded air. It was she—so beautiful, so poised, so lovable. I walked over to her. She held out her hands. I caught them. I looked into her gorgeous eyes. She gazed back. We smiled simultaneously.

What we said did not matter, for what passed in that initial longing look gave birth to a new life and love . . . at first sight. We reveled in each other's company; time and place mattered not. We were aware only of each another.

Four momentous days later, still intoxicated by the sting of the arrow, I declared my love. There was no hesitation in its appraisal and reciprocation.

We married four months later . . . a blind date materialized, a future of bliss certain.

Manny Gold

Reprinted by permission of Off the Mark and Mark Parisi. © *1999 Mark Parisi.*

The Deposit Slip

At six-foot-seven, Terry Kirk was hard to miss. Jean noticed him several times when he stopped by the bank to make deposits from his freelance photography business. Somehow, he always ended up at her window.

"May I help you?" she asked.

"Yes, I'd like to deposit these checks," he answered.

That was the extent of their conversation. *Still,* Jean thought, *he seems nice—tall but nice.*

Terry, on the other hand, never appeared to take notice of Jean. Never, that is, until he saw her in a different setting.

Terry's photography business took him to weddings, recitals, graduations—anywhere he could pick up a little money taking pictures. His job also led him to various restaurants where he photographed customers enjoying an evening out. Military guys loved to pose with their buddies, and couples snuggled together and smiled when he snapped his camera. As Terry flashed bulb after bulb, his friend and partner, Irving Riis, developed the film in a photography lab they had set up in a back room, with the black-and-white 8 x 10s ready for purchase before the patrons left.

One Friday night, the two entrepreneurs descended

upon the 1600 Club. The tables were full. Walking around the crowded restaurant with his cumbersome camera, Terry suddenly stumbled upon Jean sitting in a booth talking with her girlfriend. She looked familiar. *Where do I know her from?* Terry wondered. *Oh, yes, the bank!* He pictured the nameplate by her teller window. *Jean Dunnam—that's her name.* For some reason, she seemed different here. He had always thought her attractive but never noticed before how really pretty she was. *What a nice smile,* Terry thought, *and those deep set eyes*—her grandmother's eyes, he later learned. They took his breath away.

"Hi," he said, stopping in front of their table.

Jean looked up with a startled expression, then recognized him. "Oh, hello, Mr. Kirk," she said, smiling.

Mr. Kirk, Terry thought. *She sure is being formal. I'll have to think of something to capture her attention.* "Would you like your picture taken?" he asked.

Jean looked at her friend, who shook her head. "No, thank you," she said.

Terry moved on to the next group. *Well, I sure bowled her over with my charming personality and witty conversation,* he thought. As he walked among the tables, snapping pictures, he tried to keep Jean in sight. He had not paid too much attention to her at the bank—she was just a teller who waited on him. But here she seemed more genuine, more alive—and those eyes. He watched her unobserved as she spoke animatedly with her friend. *She's not here with a fellow. I wonder if she's attached?* Jean smiled at him as he passed by her table again. *Good! No ring.* He sighed, relieved.

When Terry made the rounds again, Jean and her friend had already left. "Now I've missed my chance," he complained to Irving when he took the next batch of undeveloped pictures to their makeshift lab. He explained about the girl from the bank.

"It's not like you don't know where to find her," his friend pointed out.

Terry could hardly wait for the bank to open on Monday. One of the first customers in the door that morning, he got in line and pondered the best way to approach Jean. *What if the head teller hears me ask her out?* Terry thought. *I might get her in trouble.* On impulse he walked to the island in the middle of the lobby and grabbed a blank deposit slip. Quickly, he wrote on it and stepped back into line.

When Jean called, "Next customer, please," and looked up to see the tall, young photographer standing in front of her, Terry thought he detected a blush spread across her cheeks.

"May I help you?" she asked.

Without saying a word, Terry handed her the note written on the back of the deposit slip, never considering that he might be mistaken for a bank robber. Startled, Jean stared at Terry for a moment, then studied the note that read:

Will you go out with me? Yes ___ No ___
What night would you like to go out? Friday ___
Saturday ___
What is your phone number? _____

Smiling, Jean filled out the note and handed it back. Thus began an eight-month courtship that ended in marriage. Well, not ended exactly. The courtship continues to this day.

Together they persevered through good times and bad. Terry worked for thirty years as medical photographer at a large private hospital. Jean stayed home to raise their three daughters and then went back to work for the bank, eventually retiring as a savings counselor.

The deposit slip, with its note on the back, still occupies a page in their scrapbook. Fifty-three years later, Terry remembers that bank transaction as the best investment he ever made.

Tracy Kirk Crump

Forever Smile

The art of love . . . is largely the art of persistence.

Albert Ellis

The dining room is filled with family. We are well-organized for this yuletide gathering, all placing our gifts under the festive nine-foot Christmas tree. In addition to the traditional decorations, a vacant chair remains in memory of Ann, my mother-in-law, who has since passed away. The celebration begins with a moment of silence; I look fondly at her chair. I bow my head.

Ann's prayer is read aloud:

> *Our father who art in heaven, we have gathered at this table, humble, grateful, and glad. We thank thee for the great miracle of life, for the exaltation of being human, for the capacity to love . . .*

I close my eyes and think back to when I met Ann. She was my patient at a dialysis clinic where I worked. She wore the sweetest smile I'd ever seen. After over a year of treatments and just before Christmas, Ann turned to me

and said, "I would like you to meet my daughter, Connie."
She held out a wallet-size picture.
"Ann! She has your smile!" I said. "If I am lucky, I'll meet
your daughter, ask her out to dinner, take her to a movie,
marry her, and give you grandchildren by next
Christmas!"

Ann quietly giggled.

A few days later, my boss, Charles, asked me if I would
work a few more hours to give a treatment to one of our
patients who had just been admitted to the coronary care
unit. It was Ann. Upon arrival, I saw that her daughter, the
one in the photo, was with her. Heat traveled all over my
body as if I had been struck by lightning. There I was, tired
and unshaven and shaken—some first impression.

"Hi, I'm Ray Duarte, your mother's nurse."

Connie smiled with relief, "Oh, thank God it's you.
Mother trusts you so much."

It seemed that Connie knew a lot about me, even
though we had never met. Evidently Ann had told her
daughter a lot about me, which made meeting Connie a
bit easier for me. Together we eased her mom through the
difficult treatment. Later that day I approached my boss.
"Charles, every time Ann needs treatment could I be her
nurse?"

He agreed.

By God's grace, Ann got well. After weeks in the hospital, she was discharged and returned to the outpatient
dialysis center, where I normally worked as the charge
nurse. The day of Ann's first treatment back from the hospital, I briefed the entire staff that if Ann's daughter,
Connie, called, to please forward it to me.

Soon after, Connie called to check on her mother.

"Oh, hello? Yes, your mom is here. I have started her
treatment, and she is doing well." With an appropriate
segue, I popped the question, asking her out for dinner.

There was a long pause; I started to feel uneasy. Finally, Connie said, "Yes, I would love to."

Connie and I were both in our thirties. She had never married. With her concerns about Mom's health, Connie had not made dating a priority. But her cousin Lucille helped out by watching Ann while Connie and I spent many weeks courting. We attended plays, dined out, and talked about all sorts of things.

I knew that Connie did not even want to hear the word *love*, so slowly and gently, after many weeks of dating, I told her how I loved her . . . smile. It all started with that wonderful smile of hers. The one she got from her mother.

One day I said, "Connie, I love you. Will you marry me?"

Silence stretched between us. A little voice inside me questioned, *My God, what did I do?*

Finally, she smiled and responded, "Ask me again later."

She took my question seriously and, more important, did not say no. Now I had to come up with clever ways of saying "I love you. Will you marry me?" I felt sure I was going to need to repeat the question many times before Connie would finally say yes.

After several failed attempts, I blurted out one night, "Connie, do you know that the word *yes* is like a smile that will last forever?" It worked!

Connie and I were married a year later. Mom got her wish and saw her only daughter marry. I insisted that Mom live with us, so that Connie and I could care for her.

I loved Ann; she gave me the greatest gift of my life. She gave her daughter to me as my soul mate. A year after Connie and I were married, Mom passed away. Ann's soul is always present with us.

The joyful screeching of children running up and down the row of tables startle me from my reminiscing. Cousin Lucille calms the children. "Shoosh, Santa is near."

I bow my head as Ann's prayer is closed:

For the wisdom of the old,
For the courage of the young,
For the promise of the child,
For the strength that comes when needed,
This family united here today, whom much is given,
much is required. May we and our children always
remember this. Amen.

The aromas of pine, cookies, and freshly brewed coffee permeates the air and adds a welcoming ambiance to a family that is now gathered in celebration. Twenty Christmases have gone by, and I'm thankful for each day. With Ann's vacant chair in close proximity, I hold Connie's hand and recollect with her that "the word *yes* is like a smile that will last forever."

Ray Duarte

Blessings from Above

*Let us be grateful to people who make us happy;
they are the charming gardeners who make our
souls blossom.*

Marcel Proust

February 14, 2000, my rocky first marriage ended in
divorce. As a result, I devised a set of standards of how a
man should treat me. I also had my twenty-two-month-
old son, Brooks, to consider, so I established criteria of a
suitable stepfather. My list of qualities that any male
suitor needed in order to date me was horrendous. It was
going to be hard for any man to get my attention.

But also on February 14, 2000, David walked into my
life. The day was indeed magical. David could barely
speak, but the look he gave me, along with his striking
smile was forever imprinted on my mind.

Two weeks after our first meeting, David and I had
lunch. Agreeing to the lunch date was my way of elimi-
nating him quickly. Much to my surprise, David was
very reserved, almost nervous. He acted as if he were

interviewing for the most important job of his life.

We talked about our families and our goals in life and how we got to where we were right then and there. I boldly told him that if I was "looking for anything, it would be someone who would treat me like a princess." After lunch, we said our good-byes; he went home, and I went back to work. David was a consultant with the company I worked for. His job meant traveling 400 miles away from his home. Crossing him off my list would be easy— or so I thought.

He stayed on my mind a lot after that first date. The fact that he attended church and that at thirty-nine years old had never been close to marriage was very appealing to me. And the way he looked at me and his smile, along with his infectious laugh, warmed my heart. It was as if God was saying, "He will always treat you like a princess." But I had firmly built my walls. If God wanted them down, then he would have to dismantle them piece by piece.

David and I began dating occasionally when he came to town on business. We ate at fancy restaurants, where we would talk and linger for hours. We talked about my thoughts on being treated like a princess as well as other "must have" qualities on my list. Sometimes we took long walks under beautiful star-filled skies. As we walked, he would often trip, paying more attention to me than on where he was going. And every time he tripped he said, "Have that removed." But his wittiness made me laugh so many times that it took the edge off my nervousness.

It wasn't long before David wanted Brooks to go out with us as well. We went to the park, the pool, the zoo, and the children's museum. David would even change Brooks' dirty diapers and read to him at bedtime.

Immediately after Easter of 2000, I traveled to his hometown to meet his parents. David's father was a conservative preacher and his mother, a realtor. I was concerned that his parents would judge me because I was a divorced, single mother.

Instead, I felt warmly received. His mother and sisters had Easter gifts for me to take home to Brooks. His mother showered me with attention and did most of the talking. As she showed me her guest room, I got the full history behind its theme—the wedding room. The queen-size bed was adorned with a white lace bedspread and fluffy antique pillows. The only portraits on the wall were of two of her three daughters in their wedding gowns in very modern settings, and a stylish old-fashioned young woman in a beautiful white gown with a lacy bodice and a full skirt. "Who is this?" I asked.

"Oh, that one? It's me," she replied dreamily. There was a long pause while we both looked at her portrait in her wedding gown. Then she turned to me with tears in her eyes and said, "We've been praying for you." Laughter overtook us as we exited the room together, arm in arm.

I am happy to say that Brooks and I accepted David's marriage proposal. We married in the fall of 2000. By this time Brooks was a two-and-a-half-year-old, active toddler. We added a special segment in the official ceremony where Brooks walked down the aisle while the wedding guests sang *Jesus Loves the Little Children*. David and I pledged to Brooks to make our family unit extra special for him and to raise him in the church. The three of us then lit the unity candle. Brooks stood patiently with my sister, his auntie Sarah, while David and I kissed.

Our loving family has grown with the addition of our daughter, Grace, in October of 2002. As a family, we dedicated her to God through baptism on February 14, 2003. This special day was threefold for our family; we will always remember God's love for each of us, our love for each other, and our love for our family unit.

Although life can be hectic, I try to tell David once a

week, if not more, "Have I told you today how much I love you?" Simply saying this to him makes us both stop and smile and remember. We remember the day we met, we remember that first lunch date, we remember our first kiss, we remember our wedding day, and we remember how God strategically placed us in each other's lives.

April Smith Carpenter

"I met Ted online. He came with a built-in family.
I got the package deal."

2

THE POWER OF LOVE

Love at first sight is easy to understand; it's when two people have been looking at each other for a lifetime that it becomes a miracle.

Amy Bloom

A Legacy of Love

True love begins when nothing is looked for in return.

Antoine De Saint-Exupéry

The year was 1950, and a young fifteen-year-old girl named Joyce fell in love. You know, the kind of love that's brand-new and exciting, full of hope and promise.

The object of her love was a tall, dark, handsome boy named Joey. Joyce and Joey met at the roller rink every Friday night. They had already exchanged rings, which they both wore around their necks on a chain—they were "going steady." They made quite a nice looking pair. Joyce's long golden hair cascaded in soft waves around her face, and her pretty red lips emphasized the most beautiful smile in the world. Joey was quite a heartthrob himself. All the girls envied Joyce. Joey and Joyce were happy, but circumstances were about to change all that.

One Friday night as Joyce was about to leave to meet Joey at the rink, her parents, Harold and Bessie, received an urgent call. Joyce's grandmother had suddenly become ill. Harold and Bessie told their seven children to pack clothes quickly so they could leave immediately to visit their grandmother in Pennsylvania. It was too late for Joyce to even call Joey to explain why she wouldn't be meeting him.

Joyce and her family made the trip from New Jersey to Pennsylvania where they stayed the weekend to care for Grandma. Joyce's parents, people of great faith, raised their children to know the love of God and the power of prayer. Joyce and her family prayed for Grandma to get well. Grandma soon recovered and regained her strength, so Joyce and her family returned home again.

The following Friday, Joyce got ready for her night at the roller rink. She couldn't wait to see Joey, since she hadn't seen him the week before. When she finally spotted Joey, her face lit up with a smile. But something was wrong. Joey skated toward her with an angry look on his face. He pulled off her ring from the chain around his neck. Without saying one word, he threw it at her and skated away. Joyce stood in disbelief, her heart broken. He wouldn't even give her a chance to explain what had happened with her grandmother.

Joyce left with tears streaming down her face. All she wanted to do was to get home, lock herself in her bedroom, and cry into her pillow. She cried for hours until the moonlight crept through her window. With tears still falling, she leaned out her windowsill. Never had her heart felt so heavy. She prayed through her tears, "Please Lord—I don't want to ever fall in love with another boy unless it's the one you want me to marry."

No sooner had she said those words when the phone rang. Her mom knocked on her bedroom door, saying the call was for her. Joyce picked up the phone and said hello but didn't recognize the voice on the other end. She heard a faint, sheepish voice say, "Is this Joyce?"

"Yes, who is this?"

"My name is Bill. You don't know me, but I saw you earlier today with your friends."

After an awkward silence, he finally asked, "Do you like country music?"

"Yeah, I guess I do. Why?"

"Oh, then listen." Bill put the phone down and started strumming his guitar, singing one song after another. Every once in a while he would manage to ask between songs, "Did you like that one?"

Bill was painfully shy and didn't have enough courage to carry on a conversation with her, but he could sing. After an hour, Bill mustered up enough courage to ask, "Joyce, will you go to the movies with me next weekend?"

Joyce answered, "I don't even know you. How old are you?"

"Fifteen."

Joyce thought there was something very sweet about this boy, even though she didn't know him at all. Finally, she said to him, "Well, I guess if you come and meet my parents, and they say it's okay, then I'll go to the movies with you."

"Okay, great. I'll walk to your house next Saturday. I'll be there at one o'clock."

The next Saturday Joyce woke up early and finished all her chores. After she got ready, she went outside on the front porch to wait. *How strange,* she thought to herself, *I'm out here waiting on my porch for someone I've never met before, and I don't even know what he looks like.*

She grew more nervous by the minute. Finally, looking down the street she noticed three boys walking toward her. Now she really grew curious, wondering which one was Bill. The boy in the middle was extremely skinny and young looking. Younger than fifteen she thought to herself. *Could that be Bill?*

When the three boys arrived, Joyce asked, "Are one of you Bill?"

The skinny boy in the middle nervously looked down at his feet, and said, "I am."

But Bill was so shy he couldn't bear the thought of going inside to meet Joyce's parents. Joyce's brother, who waited outside with her, said, "You went through this much trouble to find our phone number, call Joyce on the phone, ask her on a date, which she accepted having never met you, and now you're too shy to meet our parents?" With that her brother picked up Bill by the seat of his pants and carried him into the house. After quick introductions, her parents gave permission for them to go to the movies.

Each night thereafter, Bill called Joyce on the phone and talked for hours. He finally admitted to Joyce that he was only thirteen years old! He told her he had lied about his age because he couldn't risk her rejecting him before agreeing to at least meet him. He described to Joyce how he watched her among a crowd of girls and immediately fell in love with her beautiful smile. He needed to meet her. It was the same day she had cried out to God through her tears and prayed a simple prayer.

Joyce and Bill became inseparable. They dated for five years. Bill was not quite eighteen when he told Joyce that he wanted to marry her. He told her how he had dreamed of a wonderful life together filled with love and happiness and a house full of children. Joyce shared the same dreams. They married in July of 1955 and went on to have five children. I am one of those children.

Mom and Dad always struggled financially, but there was never a lack of love in our house. All our friends became like adopted kids, and were always welcome at family gatherings. Mom and Dad believed the more the merrier! Our family's incredible love extended to those whom others found "unlovable." Dad taught us that everyone had some good in them and that it was our job to bring it out.

He taught us that the power of love was so strong that it could overcome just about anything. He also taught us that a good book held the power to take us places in our minds that we might never explore otherwise. He taught us the beauty of music and the power of words and the power of a loving heart.

Unfortunately, at the young age of fifty-two, Dad developed a serious heart condition. Medicines and an implanted defibrillator took its toll on Dad. He lived with this condition for ten years. Although his body began failing him, Dad never grew bitter or felt sorry for himself. Instead his love for his family grew stronger. Occasionally, he spent months at a time in the hospital. The nurses and hospital staff came to know and love him. His incredible spirit touched so many lives.

Dad passed away at the age of sixty-two, and not a day goes by that I don't think of him. At about the same time Dad passed away, I started scrapbooking. During my time of grieving, I decided to work on a heritage book. At first it was hard. Many a tear fell on my page layouts! But it was through the process of telling Mom and Dad's story in a scrapbook that my grief turned into joy. I realized the depth of their love for each other and that love is eternal. Its memory sustains my family and me.

It was my mission to tell the story of Joyce and Bill and how blessed and grateful I am that I experienced firsthand their deep and enduring love for each other. By preserving their story in a scrapbook, their love can serve as an example for my children and future generations. And to think it all began with the heartfelt prayers of a young fifteen-year-old girl. Thanks, Mom . . . and thanks for the legacy, which I can now share with all those who come after me.

J. Jody Wilcox

The New Odd Couple

We need not think alike to love alike.

Francis David

We have been dating for several years, and we knew from the beginning we could not live with each other. Our daily schedules and housekeeping habits differed. Not only differed—were unacceptable to each other.

We overlook as much as we can. Now and then one of us does something the other cannot tolerate, not for one more time, not for one more minute. That is when we appreciate the fact we each can walk out the door and go home.

I leave the keys in my doorknob. He can't understand that. "Why don't you put them on the key hook?" he asks.

"I don't know. I just feel better when they're in the doorknob."

He washes his clothes every Sunday morning at exactly 6:30 and shops for food on Friday, every Friday—rain, shine, or hurricane.

I wash my clothes when I have none left to wear and

shop when I find the refrigerator is empty.

"Why do you do that?" he asks.

"Because I always did," I respond.

Our eating habits are even different. He eats prepared frozen foods. He never knows what he will eat until he reaches into his freezer. I know in the morning what I am going to eat that night. I cook everything fresh. My diet is limited and so is my cooking. Everything goes into one pot and is boiled. I haven't turned on the oven in two years.

When we eat together, he busily sets the table, making certain we have napkins and adequate silverware and a separate dish for dessert. By the time he completes this process, I am finished gulping down my supper.

When we get into the car, he reminds me to fasten my seat belt and lock the door. I do this obediently. In my own car, I drive with the doors unlocked and the seat belt hanging somewhere to the side.

He gets an A in housecleaning. Each week, he does one room. He enjoys cleaning his apartment. I know the room he will clean each week. It is reassuring to know that on a Thursday, perhaps with a hurricane nearby, or a catastrophe occurring on the other side of the world, he's cleaning the kitchen. I, on the other hand, prefer to do everything at once. And the mood needs to coincide with the chore.

We are as different from each other as possible.

We understand this about our relationship. Both in our seventies, we spent a long time developing our personal habits and our household schedules, and neither of us has any intention of changing. And we know better than to try to change each other.

Except recently, when an issue arose between us and neither of us could back away. Every now and then he insists on wearing maroon shorts with red socks. I found it impossible to concentrate on anything when he wore this ghastly combination. I told him I couldn't stand those socks together with those shorts one more time. He said, "This is the way I like it."

I have an aversion to the kitchen overhead light turned on even when it is a cloudy, sunless day. I prefer soft lamplight. On one such day, he kept turning on the overhead light. I kept turning it off. He said he couldn't see. I said, "This is the way I like it."

Because we keep an intellectual rapport, because we connect in a special way, and because true friendship is a treasure and the relationship is worth saving, he no longer wears the maroon shorts with red socks, and I no longer object when he turns on the overhead light on a cloudy, sunless day.

Even at our age, we can enjoy change.

Harriet May Savitz

One Soul, Two Bodies

Aristotle once said, "A friend is a single soul dwelling in two bodies." I never forgot those words, which my soul mate scribbled down and gave to me one afternoon many years ago. The day after the holiday season, he had returned with a somber look on his face to our college dorm room. His words stunned me: "I flunked out." Shocked, I watched as he packed his things. Could this mark the end of a remarkable bond between us?

We'll stay in touch, we promised. How often do we make such a promise? And how often do such promises fade, like leaves on a college campus in the fall? Yet, perhaps once in a lifetime we find a soul mate; something clicks between us and never dies, even when a vast ocean separates us, as it did my friend and me.

We had stayed up all night studying, walked each other home after raucous college parties, and consoled each other over women who had gotten away. And we discovered that we had had the same kind of childhoods, although separated by miles and different towns. The Beatles, the Three Stooges, the school bullies: we autonomously shared these things. Together, we had grown into young men.

Packed, he shook my hand and offered me something. I took it and turned away, not wanting to show any emotion. Glancing at the bookmark he had given me, I read Aristotle's words. That was our friendship: one soul, two bodies.

We managed to stay in touch. On a trip to England I met a young Swiss girl and fell fatally smitten. A few years later we married. We lived on the other side of the Atlantic from my friend. Still, our friendship continued through phone calls, letters, and visits. During one phone conversation, I blurted out, "Remember Aristotle and what you wrote to me that day you left our dorm room? You and I are soul mates, not meant to be separated by an ocean. I don't know how, but somehow we will be near each other again." I wasn't sure what I meant by the remark; it just slipped out. How true it would become.

On a visit one summer when we were both firmly in midlife, he met my Swiss sister-in-law and, believe it or not, fell in love as I had with her sister over twenty years before. A year later we stood together in a centuries-old chapel, and I officiated at the wedding of my sister-in-law and my best friend. In Switzerland, the husband adds his wife's maiden name to his, so now my soul mate and I share part of the same hyphenated last name. We strolled through the quaint villages, enjoyed a glass of local wine, and marveled at the miracle of friendship.

If you are lucky enough to find a soul mate in life, hold on to him or her, even if an ocean keeps you apart. One soul. Two bodies. Ari was right.

Arthur Bowler

Valentine

In third grade, Kirby Hanson gave me a valentine with a picture of a fuzzy lamb that said "I love ewe." He had carefully printed "I really do" and surrounded his name with *x*'s and *o*'s. My heart pounded, my cheeks reddened. I sat at my desk undone by true love. Then I found out he had given the same card to five other girls. Valentine's Day hasn't been the same since.

In high school I dated a guy who conveniently dumped me right before Valentine's Day. I got back together with him only to be dumped the week before Christmas. I guess he had gift-avoidance issues.

On our first Valentine's Day as a married couple, my husband, Derek, came home with a heart-shaped balloon. No card. I cried. He still gets a little anxious each February. And no wonder.

After that shaky start, Derek has never forgotten to present me with a card and usually chocolates or flowers, too. No more balloons.

As I slip into bed after a late-night writing session, his muffled snores fill the room. He scoots over and embraces me as he has done night after night for twenty years. I remember how he held me just like this the night my dad died. I knew I could survive my loss with Derek beside me.

I remember the night we came home from the hospital where our newborn son lay critically ill. I had held it together for two days, but the empty cradle at the foot our bed was too much. Derek held me. His tears mingled with mine, and I knew no matter what we had to face, we would face it together.

I like a mushy card.

I adore See's chocolates.

But the faithful love of the man emitting earth-shaking snores on the pillow next to mine is the best valentine of all.

Cindy Hval

"I'd like a dozen 'forgive-me-pleases.'"

Second Honeymoon Magic

If I never met you, I wouldn't like you. If I didn't like you, I wouldn't fall in love with you. If I didn't fall in love with you, I wouldn't miss you. But I did, I do, and I will.

Source Unknown

"Alex," I squealed, "the tickets came." The manila envelope I held contained the itinerary for our second honeymoon—a cruise to the Virgin Islands.

"That's nice," he mumbled, absorbed in the Saturday morning paper. I strolled over to the love seat, plopped down, and spread the envelope's contents on my lap. Alex stayed focused on the business section. I glanced at the brochure, reading the ship's itinerary out loud. He ignored me and sipped his coffee. I pretended not to notice the scowl on his face.

His disheartening response was one of the reasons I wanted this vacation. We had married ten years ago. At our wedding, Alex bragged about having lots of children. We searched for the right house with extra bedrooms.

Then we started trying to conceive, but I didn't get pregnant. I finally consulted a physician, and later even Alex gave in to some tests. When the doctor informed us there'd never be any children, I saw Alex flinch.

This reality took a toll on our marriage, although he said he didn't blame me. But he grew quieter each time a coworker, friend, or relative welcomed a baby into their lives. I suggested adoption, but he wouldn't discuss it. Nine years had passed, and these last few months we'd hardly spoken except to argue.

I planned to change all that on our seven-day cruise. The ship was scheduled to depart the following Friday, and I purchased a wardrobe to inspire him. By walking four miles every day and paying special attention to my diet, I even lost the ten pounds I'd gained over the years.

When we first met, he used to compliment me on an expensive perfume I wore. So I splurged and purchased a bottle. I tried to think of everything to make this special for us. I needed to believe this cruise would improve our relationship. I carefully counted down the days.

On Thursday afternoon, I hummed as I packed. Alex's suitcase was propped next to the bed, empty. The telephone rang. It was Alex.

"Victoria, something's come up . . . Jackson quit today. We're shorthanded. So I can't leave tomorrow."

"But, Alex, can't someone else cover? It's our second honeymoon. We planned this months ago." I bit my bottom lip.

"The boss needs me. It's a great chance for me to show him my stuff. So don't wait up, I'm pulling a double." He hung up. Prickles stirred on my neck while tears stung my eyes.

Depressed, I washed the dishes and folded the last load of laundry. I thought if I kept myself busy, I would cure my disappointment. It didn't work. I went to bed crying myself to sleep.

Alex crept in beside me after midnight. That morning, when I awakened, he had already gone. A scribbled note sat on the table. It read, "Have fun. Alex." I noticed he didn't sign it "Love, Alex." I brushed away new tears. Looks like I would be taking my second honeymoon alone. A cold knot formed in my stomach.

I tossed a box of tissues into my suitcase and snapped it shut. Alex chose his job over me. The magic had disappeared from our marriage, and I just lost any chance of recovering it. The tickets were nonrefundable, so thinking positively, I abandoned Alex's on the table.

I dialed his office to give him one last chance and heard a woman's cheery voice answer. "Is Alex Montgomery there?" I stammered.

"He's right here," she gushed. I recognized the flirtatious tone in her voice. An icy fear tugged my heart.

"Alex Montgomery."

"I just wanted to say good-bye, unless . . ."

"Have a good time. Lots of women go alone. You'll make some friends. If things ease up here, I'll meet up with you."

As he said good-bye, I heard giggles in the background. My throat tightened. Was he having an affair? He had acted distant the last few weeks and had worked too many late nights. My insides cringed as I deposited my wedding band on top of his ticket. As I shut the door, I resolved to leave my misery behind, at least for the length of the cruise.

I drove myself to the dock, wrestled with my suitcase, and joined the line. I watched lots of couples check in. I handed my ticket to the man behind the counter.

"Mrs. Montgomery, there are two passengers listed in cabin 443, will the other party be arriving before the ship departs?"

"No. My husband had an emergency at work. I'm going alone." Loneliness stabbed my heart, the attendant smiled at me with a sympathetic look on his face.

"We have eight hundred passengers on this cruise. There are plenty of others traveling by themselves. Enjoy the Caribbean, Mrs. Montgomery."

"Thanks." I boarded the ship, posed for a picture, and wandered to my cabin. The room, smaller than I imagined, had two portholes. I plunked down on the bed. I felt my heart twisting inside. How different it would be if Alex were here. When had he grown tired of me? Swallowing hard, I resolved to stop wallowing in self pity. The purpose of this trip was to revitalize myself, with or without Alex. I unpacked my suitcase and dressed for dinner.

The first night, I met a man named Paul seated next to me in the dining room. He said he had a small business and was a widower. Everything about him seemed first-class. We ordered the seven-course dinner and had lots of time to get acquainted. As the evening progressed, I realized he was flirting with me. Alex said I'd make friends; wouldn't he be surprised! When Paul walked me to my cabin, he asked if he could accompany me on the next day's tour. Flattered, I agreed.

When the ship docked, we stood with the excited throng of passengers waiting to exit. I inhaled the salt-scented sea breeze and watched the aqua waves slap at the beach.

Paul and I toured the tropical island together and dined at a local pub. His enchanting attention helped ease my unhappiness, but I longed for Alex. Paul lifted my spirits, but only as a friend. When he gently kissed my cheek that night, I found I missed Alex even more.

The next evening, Paul accompanied me to the show in the ballroom. Afterward, I planned on telling him that I couldn't see him anymore. I smiled briefly before the lights dimmed; he'd make some lucky woman a nice husband.

The ballroom surrounded a curved center stage. The

orchestra started and several costumed dancers whirled across the floor. Then came a comedy duo, followed by the cruise director, who introduced the main act.

The spotlight illuminated a magician dressed in a black suit and cape. His quick routine brought a flurry of *oohs, aahs,* and loud clapping. For the last trick of the evening, he included his slim assistant. She climbed into a cube-shaped box; he closed the lid and padlocked it. He said a few words, waved his wand, and then reopened the box. It was empty. The applause grew louder as he angled it for each segment of the audience to view. He locked the box for the second time; a hush settled over the crowd.

"Is there a Mrs. Victoria Montgomery in the audience?" the magician asked. His voice echoed through the ballroom.

I raised my hand and squirmed in my seat. Paul turned and stared at me. "I'm married," I whispered. "I planned on telling you after the show. I'm sorry."

"So am I," he answered. Paul blushed and slid out of his seat, then escaped down the aisle.

"Please, stand, this trick is dedicated to you." The magician waved his wand over the cube and said, "Abracadabra." He released the locks and opened the lid. A tall husky man popped out. Not just any man; it was Alex! Adrenaline rushed through me.

The magician announced, "Surprise! Happy tenth anniversary to Mr. and Mrs. Montgomery!" Everyone clapped. Alex jogged to join me in the third row. He settled into the empty seat, a wide smile on his face.

He kissed me tenderly.

"What happened? How did you . . . ?"

"Poof, I'm here. It took me two days to get a flight. We still have five days. If you let me, I promise to make them perfect."

"I thought you had to work and impress the boss."

"Forget the boss. When I found your ring with my ticket, I thought I'd lost you. Nothing's worth that."

"Things will have to be different, Alex. You can't shut me out anymore."

"Okay, okay. Let's start over. All I know is I missed you."

Alex withdrew my wedding band from his pocket and asked, "Will you marry me—again, fine lady?"

"Yes," I whispered, and he slipped the ring on my finger. I waved my hand and said, "Abracadabra, you're eternally under my spell, Mr. Montgomery."

"There's no place I'd rather be. And we have an appointment to fill out an adoption application when we get home."

"Wow," I said. The second honeymoon magic I'd wished for was really coming true.

Suzanne Baginskie

"And do you promise that your schedules will, please put your Blackberry away, never be more important than your times together?"

Milestones

Just before dawn, I hear the sound of dresser drawers opening and closing. I know he is getting ready for another twenty-four-hour shift. His is a demanding job, filled with grave responsibilities and risks. Whenever he leaves for work, I remember receiving an early morning call some years ago, saying he had been seriously injured, and the choking feeling I had when I considered I might lose him.

Soon he leans over to kiss me. "I'm gone," he says, leaving me with the scent of his cologne as he wrestles his colossal sports bag out the bedroom door.

As he disappears into the darkness to join the suburban commuters, I think back to the first time I watched him leave for work dressed in his blue fire department uniform. He helps keep the citizens safe, he said, but it did little to console me. I cried half the day and ached for him in the night.

For a few more minutes, I lie perfectly still with my thoughts. This month marks our twentieth wedding anniversary, and I want to remember my marriage to him all these years.

From the time I was a young girl, I dreamed of a garden wedding. It would occur during the cool of the day, under a shade of trees, with a handful of witnesses. Potted yellow flowers would nod to me as I swept by them on the way to the arms of my beloved.

For a while it seemed my dream would wash away. A hurricane named Allen brewed in the Gulf of Mexico. Forecasters predicted it to make landfall the very day of our wedding. It didn't help matters that the hurricane's name matched my last name. We endured endless jokes over that one.

But, incredibly, our special day brought not so much as a sprinkle on the happy wedding party.

The day after was another matter altogether. Wind and rain pounded against our hotel window for hours. As we were typical newlyweds, the weather forecast didn't interfere much with our plans anyway. San Antonio never looked better.

Early on in our marriage, it was clear that he dreamed of journeying coast-to-coast, strolling along distant beaches, and sipping gourmet coffee in cafés nestled in the shadows of mountain peaks. He taught me about maps and compasses and sundials.

As time and duties allowed—usually once a year—he charted a course that carried us to fascinating and enchanting places. I remember pink sunsets along Florida's Emerald Coast, gathering rocks from a cold creek in the Great Smoky Mountains, riding the Spirit of Vicksburg down the mighty Mississippi River, marveling at autumn's palette in upstate New York, sleeping under the stars at the foot of the Appalachian Mountains, and staring in silent wonder at the sights and sounds of Niagara Falls.

Many nights I discovered him fast asleep on the sofa, a road atlas pressed against his chest. I dared not wake him.

I knew he was dreaming of secluded log cabins and old landmarks in ancient cities.

After the birth of our daughter, I had a crazy idea: I would stay at home to raise our child, and I would write. Not just write, but get paid to write! Clearly, it was not the most thrilling thing he had ever heard, but it was my dream, so he went along.

Neither of us realized that I would swim against the tide. And just when it seemed I would drown in rejection letters, I found a few editors who gave me a chance. The tide turned. Every time my byline appeared in magazines and newspapers, I don't know whose smile was wider, his or mine.

One day I got a call from a publishing house. My first book-length manuscript had been accepted for publication. We danced in circles across the kitchen floor, singing "Cel-e-brate good times, come on!"

Through the years, I have learned that marriage is not just about celebrating the good times; it is also about sharing the agony. Being together hasn't always been satisfying. Neither has it always been comfortable.

At times our lives have been filled with tremendous loss and pain. We have lived through serious illnesses and major surgeries, through years of trying to conceive a child, and the dissension that comes with it. We've mourned the deaths of mothers and fathers, and we have been outraged at the negligence of a doctor who almost took the life of our only child. We've known the anguish that comes when precious heirlooms disappear at the hands of a thief. We've nursed broken ankles, broken toes, broken shoulders, and broken hearts. We've engaged in bitter quarrels and endured excruciating marriage counseling. There were times when it would have been so much easier to walk away—and times when we almost did.

But even when we dragged suitcases from closets and fled in anger, I knew it was not the end. All we needed was time. Time to sit a spell and reexamine this thing called *marriage,* and think about that enchanted summer evening when we vowed to be there for each other—in sickness and in health, for better or worse. It was this—the memory of a sacred promise—that bridged the gulf between us. It is what kept us together when our love seemed elusive.

Looking back, the arrival of a hurricane on our wedding day somehow seems appropriate. For we certainly encountered our share of storms. But it feels good knowing we survived—knowing we were at times in serious trouble but did whatever it took to stay together.

Sometimes all it takes to live through a hurricane is to call for help. You wade through deep water and crawl into a rescue boat. You cling to each other and find a safe place until the worst is over. Whatever destruction the storm leaves in its wake, you know that—together—you will summon the strength to repair and rebuild.

So dream on, my beloved. Dream of bustling cities and isolated villages. Dream of sailing on sapphire seas and riding horseback through dusty canyons. I'll be there in your dreams. Together we'll walk along summer beaches, then dance under an autumn moon until forever begins.

Dayle Allen Shockley

Never Thought

Never thought I could love a guy any more,
Than at thirteen, sharing a first kiss.
Never thought I could love a guy more,
Than at sixteen, dancing at the prom.
Never thought I could love a guy more,
Than at twenty, saying, "I do."
Knew I'd never love a guy more,
Than watching the tears course down his cheeks,
As he gently held our daughter,
For the very first time.

Sabrina A. Taylor

My First and Last Roses

Let all thy joys be as the month of May
And all thy days be as a marriage day. . . .

Francis Quarles

Like most young girls, I always dreamed of a guy sending me flowers. I will never forget when this dream came true. Mine were not delivered by a florist, but by my beau, Terry. In fact, he hid them in my locker on Valentine's Day. I will never forget how tickled I felt as I kissed his blushing face.

In the years that followed, Terry sent me countless beautiful flowers as our love blossomed. Nevertheless, after seven years of courting, as well as seven years of marriage, I no longer receive his flowers. Not for any sad reason, not for financial reasons, but to mark a precious memory.

As I held my beautiful newborn baby daughter, Savannah, a nurse walked into my room, carrying a beautiful bouquet of a dozen perfectly pink roses. I thought she had made a mistake. They couldn't possibly be mine. I had never received a dozen roses at one time, and the color was wrong; Terry's roses were always red, never pink!

As I read the card, there was no mistaking my husband's handwriting as well as his heart. His words will be forever treasured in my heart:

> To My Beautiful Girls
>> I love you both so very much
>
> Terry
> (I mean Dad!)

I smiled at his addition of the word *Dad*. Like the roses changing from red to pink and his signature from Terry to Dad, our love for each other was no longer shared by just us two. Our love could now be seen in this wonderful being I cuddled in my arms.

Usually with change comes uncertainty of the unknown. Since our teenage dating years, we always knew that children would be included in our wonderful life with each other.

Looking at the word *Dad* once more, my tears began to flow. We had previously suffered a heartbreaking miscarriage, countless trips to the doctors, seemingly endless tests, and disabling drug therapy. No longer did these important sacrifices compare to this privilege of my husband signing this simple but special three-letter word. This wonderful man had prayed with me when I had asked him to leave me because I could not give him children. He said that we could always adopt children, but he could not adopt me.

Peeking his head into my hospital room, my husband's blushing face reminded me of that shy teenage boy that had stolen my heart on Valentine's Day fourteen years ago. As I once again kissed his blushing face, I could not help but notice the pink flowers matched his face as well as the beautiful and perfectly round face of our daughter. I smiled at the thought that Savannah's first dozen roses came from her sweet daddy. It was the first dozen roses for Savannah as well as her mother. But more important, it was the first time Terry was blessed to write that priceless three-letter word—*Dad.*

This precious memory does not need to be frozen in time, because it will warm a very special place in my heart for eternity.

On Valentine's Day, as well as many other special occasions, florists are busy arranging their beautiful flowers, particularly roses. Nevertheless, you will never find them making an arrangement for me. I have already been given the most beautiful roses on the most perfect day of my life.

What else could a woman want?

Why mess with perfection?

Stephanie Ray Brown

$\overline{3}$

GRATITUDE

If I know what love is, it is because of you.

Hermann Hesse

A Hand to Hold

"My dear, you are so lucky. I used to have what you have."

The well-dressed elderly lady seated in the church pew next to me took me quite by surprise as she leaned in and spoke to me following the Sunday service. Somewhat befuddled, I managed to utter a quiet thank you, although at that instant I was a little unsure of the meaning behind her words. *What did I possess that this obviously well-off woman did not?* Strands of pearls adorned her neck, and I could not help but notice the many sparkling gemstones that graced her aging fingers.

As I looked down at my own hands, the answer became apparent. Interlocked in my hand was the hand of my husband. Listening to the sermon together on Sunday mornings had led us to a natural closeness to God and to each other. More often than not, my husband would reach for my hand during the sermon or put his arm around mine during the time of silent prayer and reflection. This time together was sacred to us in more than just the obvious way. With our two young daughters in their Sunday school rooms, we reconnected and recharged after a hectic week of work, playgroups, and diaper changes.

When I looked across the pew at the woman next to me, I realized that she sat alone. Most likely, the husband whose hand once held hers on Sunday mornings had passed on and left her with the memories of what I now share with my husband. "I am so lucky," I whispered to her in reply. As I stood up and prepared to leave the church, I looked up at my husband, Allen, and smiled. What I have with him is indeed a special blessing.

As a thirty-something, stay-at-home mom, I relish the opportunity to talk with other women my age and swap stories about our young children. However, when the topic turns from life in the preschool carpool line to complaints about spouses, I become uncharacteristically mute. Stories of husbands who do not equally contribute to child care or housework are commonplace. The same holds for the husbands who travel for days (weeks, months . . .) on end and have little energy left over for romance or family.

After seven years of marriage, I now realize that I am an especially lucky woman!

My husband, Allen, once an executive with all the pressures of long commutes, business trips, and the very real possibility of transferring across the country, away from my close-knit extended family, made the difficult decision to resign from his high-powered job. He now owns his own small business in our hometown. Instead of executive perks, he now gets to see the perky antics of our two little girls as we eat lunch together every day. Rather than coming home from work after 7:00 PM, Allen is home like clockwork for our nightly six o'clock family dinner. Like every household with young children, much work is left for the post-dinner hour. We draw baths, read stories, and wash the dishes. Instead of retreating to the world of ESPN or pretending to tinker with something "manly" in the garage or basement, my husband is right by my side as we complete the nightly household tasks.

When weekends roll around, I am the blessed woman who does not need to cook a single meal. Warm maple syrup and hazelnut coffee aromas waft upward from our kitchen as Allen prepares breakfast and allows me the luxury of lingering in a hot shower. This wonderful man does not hesitate to give me a much-needed break whenever I want to go shopping or out to lunch with friends. When I return I find snowmen in our yard, LEGO castles in our playroom, and my two sweet princesses wearing paper crowns that Daddy cut out for them to wear.

"Dad made us a teddy bear picnic while you were at Target!" my four-year-old excitedly exclaims as I enter the door, loaded down with shopping bags.

"We had real food! Pretzels and raisins on the big blanket!"

I am given alone time to shop and socialize sans diaper bags, but my children are the recipients of the real gift . . . time spent with their amazing father.

The man who irons all of our clothes, cooks, cleans, and wraps every Christmas present (honestly, all I do is put on the sticky bows and gift tags!) is also generous with his affection toward me. After the children are asleep, I often find myself sitting in front of a warm fire or a few lit candles. Herbal tea is served to me as we discuss our children's latest antics or our hopes for the future.

I realize that the elderly lady in church was quite correct. What I possess is truly special. I am the luckiest woman in the world to be blessed with such a caring, giving husband. Through the words of a complete stranger, I am reminded to cherish each moment with the man I love. I fully intend to keep his hand intertwined in mine for as long as God allows.

Stefanie Wass

Gotcha! And I'm Glad

How ow lucky I am to have something that makes saying good-bye hard.

From the movie *Annie*

Still wearing my shapeless blue nightgown, and my hair a tangled nest, I pecked Mike good-bye as he left for work. Mike waved in return, a rushed gesture over his shoulder. I shook my head. *Whatever happened to the passionate good-byes, the loving, lingering embraces?*

No time for that now. The kids thumped down the stairs.

"Mom, I can't find my sneaker," called Andy.

"Can you sign this permission slip?" asked Kate.

In a tumble of activity, I helped the kids get off to school and then finally sat down at the computer to start my day. I worked from home and sometimes didn't bother getting dressed until noon. My green fuzzy slippers were hardly provocative, I realized. But comfortable. Like my marriage?

Mike and I had been married for twenty-four years— happy years. Sure, things weren't always as exciting as the day we had met, two young college kids on a starry night. We'd spent so many romantic times together: long walks, movies, dances. But the most romantic thing of all was Mike's cards.

I still had all of Mike's cards tied with a satin ribbon and tucked inside a shoe box. The very first card he ever gave me was blue with two white cartoon figures sporting goofy smiles. Across the top it read "GOTCHA." Inside it continued: ". . . AND I'M GLAD." How many times did we repeat this silly phrase to each other through our own goofy grins?

After that came many more cards—funny cards, romantic cards, and messages of love and hope for the future. He always made sure to send his cards through the mail, even if we were separated by only a few campus blocks. Knowing he took the time and effort to get a stamp and post the correspondence made receiving that card all the more special.

The cards continued after we married, birthdays and anniversaries included. "We'll get through it . . . together," he once wrote on a card of encouragement sent from his work to home. And I knew we would. Sometimes he sent me cards out of the clear blue sky. "Thinking of you today." Opening those cards was like opening a door to my heart.

But as I shuffled a huge stack of papers on my desk, I wasn't thinking of the cards. I was just thinking about how much work I needed to do.

Around midday I took a break from my computer work and began straightening the kitchen. *So many dishes to do. What should I make for dinner?* Soon the kids would be home. I had many little details to think about, and the last thing on my mind was romance. That's why I was surprised when I went to the mailbox that day and noticed Mike's familiar handwriting on a piece of mail.

I put down my dishcloth and slipped the card out of its envelope. On the front of the card was a picture of two scruffy dogs sprawled across a couch, lazy and peaceful—just like Mike and me. We were comfortable together, true, but we also shared something deeper. A true, meaningful relationship that was busy and full. And when I thought about it, that deep, abiding love could be romantic. I just needed to take the time to remember.

I smiled, staring at the card for a long time. My heart felt warm and full as I traced the letters with my finger. Apart from his signature, there were no words inside. But there didn't have to be. I knew everything he wanted to say: "Gotcha . . . and I'm glad." And when Mike came home from work, I'd be sure he knew that I was glad, too.

Peggy Frezon

"Remember when we used to mail
personal love notes? Now they just text each other."

The Precious Package

You don't love someone for their looks, or their clothes, or for their fancy car, but because they sing a song only you can hear.

Source Unknown

When Eric woke up one night in November 2002 with severe chest pains, I immediately called an ambulance. In 1990 he had suffered a mild heart attack, but with medication he had experienced no problems since.

By the time the ambulance arrived, his pains had receded, but the EMTs wired him up to the heart monitors and drove us the forty miles to our nearest hospital. Eric looked well and chatted with the medic about golf.

We suspected that this episode would result in only an alteration to Eric's medication.

Eric had tests on Saturday and called me on Sunday afternoon. "They don't seem all that happy, so they are keeping me in another couple of days to get me on the treadmill."

A warning bell rang that maybe this wasn't as simple as we thought. For the first time, I began to worry about Eric.

Married for thirty years, we are very close and I missed him. We have no children but do have three cats. They kept looking behind me whenever I came inside, as if saying, "Well, where is he?"

On the day of his treadmill test, I waited in his hospital room. When they brought him back, he just looked at me and quietly said, "It's not good news, Toots." He bit his lip, then said, "It's a triple."

I stared at him. "A triple bypass?" My head went round, and I leaned on his bedside cabinet, my whole world spinning around me. Eric was dangerously ill. Despite a six-month waiting list for this operation, his doctor would not release Eric until he had the bypass surgery. We both knew this meant his condition was not stable.

I went home that night, hating to leave him alone with his worry. As I sat on the train, the night was so dark that all I could see was my reflection in the window. My tears poured down my cheeks. I just could not imagine this was happening to two people who loved each other so much.

I cried everywhere for the next few days: in the living room, in the bathroom. I didn't go to bed because I couldn't bear to lie in bed and imagine one day he might not be there beside me.

At the end of the first week, a box arrived for me from the United States. I frowned and then saw on the side "The San Francisco Music Box Company."

I had ordered a surprise Christmas present for Eric and me via the Internet. We both loved the movie *Somewhere in Time*, and when I found a small music box adorned with a carousel that played its theme, I sent for it.

I planned to put it on top of our television cabinet on Christmas morning, play it, then watch Eric's reaction. I opened the carton but was so upset that I sobbed, petrified that Eric would never hear this.

It was when I was on the floor unpacking the music box

that I began to pray. Up till then, I just asked God to make him better. Now I handed over to him the most precious package of my life. "He's in your hands now; you know how good a man he is; you know how much I love him. Please, please, make him better and bring him back to me!"

Time dragged. Eric had entered the hospital on November 15 and finally received a surgery date of December 4. Despite the worry, we were both relieved, because having this surgery was the only way he was going to be able to come home. I hurt for him because he missed so much being home, the cats, and me.

The night before his operation, I waved good-bye to him at his hospital room door and again at the elevator. But once the doors closed, I dissolved into hysterics in my friend's arms. He looked so well, and I was so scared I would never see him again. I just wanted to be with him, through the night, through the operation. Again I asked the Lord to be in my place, holding him, wrapping him up in his love, and bringing him through everything.

I saw him the next evening, and although he looked an odd color, he blinked open his lovely warm brown eyes and there was "my Eric." He worked hard at all the exercises they gave him, and by December 10 he was on his way home.

He needed to take it easy for a while, so we spent a quiet Christmas. But just as planned on Christmas day, I wound up the music box. As the little carousel went round and the theme from *Somewhere in Time* tinkled softly in our living room, I burst into tears and rushed into Eric's arms.

Often I wind up the carousel and let it play our theme. I tell Eric, "Music boxes should be used regularly, to keep them going." But it's my chance to give thanks because my "precious package" was returned to me, just as I asked.

Joyce Stark

A Man Has to Play Hard to Get Sometimes

Beauty is power; a smile is its sword.

Charles Reade

The first time I saw him, fireworks ignited and the "pop-pop-pop" went off in my heart. It wasn't the Fourth of July, but rockets exploded anyway. This high school girl never dreamed of a taller, darker, or more handsome man.

The English teacher's assignment required a research paper on lumberjacks. I didn't know anything about lumberjacks, but when I saw all the kids surrounding Emmitt in the library, I pushed my way through the crowd. Of course, he showed his distinct advantage over all of us—Emmitt's artistic talent left little room for competition. His sketch of a lumberjack could have appeared on a magazine cover.

"Will you draw one for me?" "And me?" "And me?" Everyone around him asked the same question.

"Sure!" he answered.

Not only was he handsome, but talented, too. *I've got it made,* I thought.

"Will you draw one for me?" I asked, batting my baby blues.

"No!" he said. (He winked at me several times in the hall, but I wanted him to eat his heart out . . . so I had played hard to get.) I played, all right . . . I played my cards all wrong that day.

What a put-down, and so much for my feminine charm. The fireworks dimmed that year. I kept my distance but became his secret admirer.

Imagine my excitement the next spring when he asked me to the junior/senior banquet as his date. I had to pinch myself. *Is this real, or am I dreaming?* I thought.

The basketball team went to state our senior year, and no matter where Emmitt was on the basketball court, this "All-State Center" could spot me in the crowd. The girls around me squealed with delight as they said, "Did you see Number Eleven wink at me?" I didn't say a word. He had eyes for me, and the fireworks kept going off.

We graduated from high school. I went to college, and Emmitt went off to war. "Sentimental Journey" became our theme song.

After his tenure in the army, the greatest fireworks of all happened on our wedding day. I finally caught my knight in shining armor. As I walked down that aisle, I thanked God for giving me this desire of my heart.

Through the years I have learned what really had attracted me to the man of my dreams. His loving heart had won mine early on.

A loving heart makes everyone beautiful. A loving heart goes beyond age, race, or status. A loving heart brings out the best in everyone.

I cannot remember not being in love with him. Even after fifty-seven years, it is still fireworks and the Fourth of July for me. Yes, he is older and grayer, but to me he is the same tall, dark, and handsome hero of my high school days.

I thought it impossible to love him more. I was wrong. I love him in a way I cannot explain. He is even more patient, compassionate, and loving, sacrificing for our three sons and me. He holds me in his arms and prays for me. He prays for our children and grandchildren. He is my protector, supporter, defender, cherisher, and the love of my life.

He is God's gift to me every day of the year, especially on Independence Day, because then I get to see two kinds of fireworks.

By the way, I asked him one day why he didn't draw a lumberjack for me back in high school, and he said, "Well, a guy has to play hard to get sometimes!"

Joan Clayton

What's in a Name?

The best and most beautiful thing in life cannot be seen, not touched, but are felt in the heart.

Helen Keller

My husband, Lee, and I don't always march to the same drummer. I'm a detailed perfectionist, while he's prone to jump right in and do it, "or it won't get done." And while I ponder world problems and dream of a hate-free society, he avoids deep, philosophical discussions, preferring instead light, playful banter.

I didn't, until recently, consider Lee a bona fide romantic. One exceptional time he said, "Y'know, Sue, the sweetest sound coming from your mouth is my name—Lee."

"Really?" I asked, surprised at the simplicity of his sentiment.

"Yeah," he said quite sincerely.

Shucks, I can handle that. "Okay, I'll say it more often—Lee."

A huge grin slid from one ear to the other. "Thanks," he said softly.

I kept my promise.

One sunny day I drove in from work and saw him toiling feverishly in our pansy bed. Back and neck injury-related problems long ago retired me from this particular creative pastime. *How I miss working alongside him.* Sighing, I went inside and prepared lunch.

"Hungry?" I called from the doorway, curious about his intense preoccupation amid scattered mulch and bucketed, minute-budded greenery. His concentration was nothing new, but he usually finished a planting design much quicker.

I opened my mouth to question his slow progress, but something stopped me. Probably his wrinkled brow and the near-desperate way he gauged the placement of the tiny plants.

"I'll eat later," he murmured, and proceeded to move the mulch about and redig.

After he finished, he called, "Come look at it, Sue."

I gazed at the flimsy patches of green, and started to ask, "Why?" Again, the words froze, undelivered.

"What d'ya think?" He wiped sweat from his brow, looking extremely pleased with himself.

"It's—nice," I said, squashing my disappointment that he'd not filled the bed as was his custom. I love the vibrant colors during winter's dismal days. Yet—on some level, I knew this was *not* the time to critique his work. The smile I gave him must have worked, because he gave me a quick, sweaty kiss and hug.

Heck, the important thing, I tried to convince myself, *is that he had enjoyed doing it.*

I studiously avoided looking at this fragile bed as winter set in.

In late January, my neck and back started acting up again, making getting about difficult. Depression settled over me like leaden fog. Even driving proved difficult, because rotating my neck and torso to see out the side of the car windows was excruciating. That day, on my way home from the grocery store, I nearly sideswiped an eighteen-wheeler, whose driver, red-faced and shaking a sausage-sized fist, yelled obscenities at me. It was the final straw. I burst into tears.

When I turned blindly into my drive, I braked and laid my head on the steering wheel to vent my sense of help-lessness. I tried to think of all the good things in my life: *my children, grandchildren . . . Lee.*

And my pansies. I needed a good laugh. I lifted my head to look at them. They blurred and swam in my teary vision, slowly clearing. . . .

My breath caught in my throat.

Shimmering under a golden sun, framed against our little white-railed porch, I witnessed my husband's tribute in rioting, *loving* color.

The blossoms spelled S-U-E.

Emily Sue Harvey

Circle of Love

Chance is always powerful. Let your hook always be cast; in the pool where you least expect it, there will be a fish.

Ovid

My youngest daughter, Mary, was a "bad-boy magnet" when it came to dating. Although she was always our rebel, Mary has a great work ethic, is pretty, personable to a fault, and would bring home every stray in town if she could. And, as for men, she did. She became a meal ticket for quite a few unsavory characters that she paired up with during her twenties.

As Mary approached thirty she seemed to settle down.

"There must be something wrong with me, Mom," she told me one night on the phone. "I don't want to party and go out all the time anymore."

I laughed, "Mary, I think this is what they call maturity."

The phone line went quiet for a while, so I figured she was mulling this idea over in her head.

"Okay," was her only answer, and we moved on to other topics.

About a month later, Mary called again for one of our weekly chats.

"Mom, I met this cool guy; he's a surfer, and I *really* like him," she said.

Here we go again, I thought.

I played it cool and didn't ask too many questions. I don't think I wanted to know the answers.

But Mary continued to tell me about him.

"Gary is ten years older than me, he's got a steady job, we have so much in common, and I think he may be the *one.*"

"A steady job?" I asked.

"Yeah, he's been there twelve years, and did I tell you he plays the guitar like a pro?"

A rock star wannabe, I thought. *Now, Sallie, that's really not fair. You haven't met him yet.*

Mary and Gary dated for about two years after that. We liked Gary and wondered if this was going anywhere. He was very different from the usual guys Mary dated. One day she called.

"Mom, Gary says he wants to come over and see you. Can we do dinner on Sunday?"

"Sure, I guess so. What's this about?"

"He won't tell me," Mary said. "Says it's a surprise."

Sunday rolled around, and after dinner I nodded for Gary to come with me into the den.

"So, Mary said that you want to talk to me about something."

"Yeah, actually I am going to ask Mary to marry me, and she said you have your mother's ring. I hoped to have it made into a ring for Mary. She tells me she was close to your mom and that her grandmother called her Little Mary Sunshine."

My eyes misted over. Mary remembered. My mom had passed away before Mary finished high school. I knew my daughter always held a special place in her heart.

I slipped Gary into my bedroom and opened my jewelry case. There sat my mother's silver wedding ring, smoothed down to a thin band by sixty years of wear. The etchings around the sides were hardly visible.

I could see the look of disappointment on Gary's face.

"I don't think this ring is what you're expecting. Maybe Mary was thinking of my mother's engagement ring that had a two carat diamond. My dad kept it for several years and then finally sold it. I also have a sterling silver band I got married in before Paul could afford to buy me a gold one. You're welcome to that one if you like," I offered.

Gary thanked me graciously and said he would take both rings and think about what he wanted to do. He promised to let me know. I didn't hear anymore from him and thought he would probably return them to me.

Mary and Gary eloped two weeks later. I didn't give the rings any more thought.

When the happy couple came by upon their arrival home, Mary ran up to me waving her outstretched left hand.

"Look, Mom! Look what Gary had made for me!" There on her hand was my wedding ring and my mother's wedding ring intertwined with a diamond band from Gary.

My eyes filled with tears and my heart swelled with love for this man. I knew Mary had finally found someone who would cherish her forever.

Sallie A. Rodman

A Little Scrap of Paper

Nothing is a waste of time if you use the experience wisely.

Auguste Rodin

After four long years of a debilitating illness, my mother slipped away from this world with a warm, loving circle of family around her. My father, who had been there with her every day and night through her struggle, held her hand and murmured softly in her ear how much he loved her and that she would always remain the "Most Beautiful Girl in the World."

He was my mother's rock and her strength throughout her illness and was never far from her side. As the day grew late, the family gathered around her bed, and with prayer, lifted her up to heaven in her final moments; she was at peace.

My sister found a letter in my mother's purse. It was an old scrap of paper, looking like something one might throw away. It had been read and folded and refolded many times; it was held together with tape and was more than a little worn.

It was a note my father had written over twenty years ago to my mother in his scrawled, unmistakable hand-writing. Written on December 6, 1981, on a day like any other, my father addressed it to "My Dearest Darling" and signed the note with a heart.

I can't share the contents here with you because the words are not mine to share. It was a letter written by a man to the woman he loved, and it was meant for no one's eyes but hers. There were no sonnets or rhymes, no lines of prose, just a heartfelt explanation of the depth of his love for her. A few days later, before my mother's casket closed, my father carefully folded the letter and placed it back in her hands where it belonged. There could be no doubt in this life or the next how much he loved her.

On the day of her funeral, we cried and mourned the loss of my mother, and we mourned the loss of a love between two people that had burned brightly over forty years. In the final months of her illness, there were many dark days, but my father's love for my mother shone through them all.

He gave her many gifts over the years, but how precious a gift he gave her in that one scrap of paper! To take it out any time, read it again, and know that no matter what the world threw at her, no matter how bad her day may have seemed, my mother knew *she was loved!*

Through the shared love of my parents, I was given a wonderful gift and learned an incredible lesson. We should all take the time to find a scrap of paper and a pen or pencil and write a note to others, telling them they are loved. Don't worry about spelling all the words right or even having good grammar. Don't wait to find that perfect greeting card that "says it all"—write your feelings about that person, whether it's your husband or wife, son, daughter, treasured friend, it doesn't matter.

And don't wait for a birthday, anniversary, or a holiday

to say it. Write them a note right now, and tell them how much you love them. Because you never know—a little scrap of paper could be the most treasured gift they will ever own.

David McAmis

Through the Years

Whenever I'm seated in a restaurant, I enjoy glancing at the different nooks and crannies, watching the various couples sitting at the tables and in the booths. I like to speculate about which ones are on a date with someone new or which ones are dining out with their usual partner. Being within hearing range isn't important. All that is necessary is being able to see their facial expressions.

As a young girl and then later as a teenager, I promised myself I would engage in conversation with my husband while dining out, rather than stare off into space and ignore him, as I had seen so many other couples do.

I thought, *How can they have nothing to talk about? Are they that bored, unhappy, or miserable? Have they stayed in a loveless marriage, for whatever reasons?*

I will never *be like that,* I would announce to myself in the silence of my mind. I knew it certainly wouldn't be possible ever to fall out of love with *my* knight in shining armor, whoever he may be.

Ah, the naiveté of youth! Those self-promises about love and marriage go hand in hand with the ones about what kind of mother I would emulate: I would never yell at my child in the checkout line at the grocery store; I would never allow my child to suck on a pacifier; and I would portray the perfect model of patience, love, and understanding.

Even though my life hasn't turned out the way my teenage self envisioned it, I really did find a prince of a man—the second time around, that is. In spite of recent divorce statistics, and especially those for second marriages, mine gloriously succeeded. Ron and I will celebrate our twenty-fifth wedding anniversary in February 2008.

How did we accomplish such a feat? If forced to provide a one-word answer, I would say *love*. But that, of course, is too clichéd. The reasons are as different as they are numbered. We both have a great sense of humor. We have the same religious backgrounds. We were blessed with the birth of our son. We both shared the same viewpoints on child rearing, and we overcame the obstacles that accompany a relationship involving stepchildren. In short, we both wanted to work hard to make our marriage last.

Of course, we argued about the same things most couples do. We've tried to follow the rule of never falling asleep mad. The longer we've been married, the shorter the list has become of things to disagree about. (Funny how that seems to work.) With age, and a little wisdom, we've each realized (especially me!) that we don't always have to be right.

Ron and I have always loved to make each other laugh. He has a dry wit, and I tend to act silly. I love breaking into song, usually when he least expects it, and doing crazy dances around the house. Just the other evening, after another one of our goofy dialogues, Ron turned to me and said, "Do you think Brad Pitt and Angelina Jolie act like this?" We both responded with the exact same words: "I doubt it!"

I'm not trying to paint a picture of a completely blissful life. Of course we have had times of worry and great sadness, but Ron has always come through for me. For years, I tried to establish a relationship with my estranged dad, but was unsuccessful. Ron was always there, listening when I needed him to and saying the words I needed to hear. During our second year of marriage, my oldest sister died at the age of forty-six from a brain tumor. Again Ron listened, comforted, and held me while I shed many tears.

Although he isn't the kind of man who shares many of his inner thoughts, I, too, am there for him. Whether it's making his favorite chocolate chip fudge cake with double fudge frosting or traveling for hours and hours by car because he refuses to fly, I'm with him.

We care about each other's feelings by giving and taking. And since I live only one time on this Earth, I'll be eternally grateful that when dining out with my wonderful husband, I've never, ever stared off into space.

Becky Povich

4

OVERCOMING OBSTACLES

The web of our life is of mingled yarn, good and ill together.

William Shakespeare

With *This* Ring?

This wasn't my first marriage, so I should know this proposing stuff by heart. But as a typical male, chances were good that I would struggle through how and when to propose to my girlfriend, Dahlynn.

We dated for several months—and knew each other for many years. We both assumed we would marry, although the date and circumstances still resided in the great unknown void of "We'll talk about that later when we have more time." Things began to change when we were strolling through our friends' jewelry store in Old Town Folsom, where the many shops fill historic brick buildings leftover from California's gold rush days.

I'm not a connoisseur of fine jewelry, or even of cheap jewelry. The fact that most of the gold and diamond rings in the store's cases were antiques meant nothing to me except that the original owners likely paid significantly less for them new than I was going to pay for any of them used one hundred years later.

Even though we stepped into the store just to browse, Dahlynn quickly spotted her perfect wedding ring. I agreed; the ring was beautiful, and, yes, I was crazy in love with her, but neither of us mentioned purchasing it. After all, I had not officially proposed to her, so buying a ring that day was not part of my planned proposal process.

Finding the perfect ring that Dahlynn loved did spur me to begin planning my proposal. I thought it would be great if I could surprise her by purchasing the ring. I returned to the jewelry store alone a few days later and wandered over to the antique wedding ring case. I scanned the display case for Dahlynn's special ring—and scanned some more. I thought, *Oh, no, these rings all look alike! Now what do I do?*

The same two women who had helped Dahlynn "choose" her special ring earlier that week were working, but their memories were as fuzzy as mine about which ring, in a case filled with antique diamond wedding rings, held Dahlynn's special ring. I left in a bit of a panic, hoping it hadn't already been sold.

The following evening, Dahlynn and I "just happened" to return to Folsom for dinner. Afterward, I suggested we go for a walk past all the antique shops. Dahlynn was tired and it actually took a bit of persuasion. As we approached the jewelry store, I steered Dahlynn inside and over to the antique wedding ring case. I planned to get her to show the salesladies and me which ring she had wanted. Unfortunately, she wasn't being very cooperative since we hadn't yet talked about a ring, let alone a wedding. Even the salesladies tried to help me persuade Dahlynn to identify *her* ring—if it was still there.

Reluctantly, Dahlynn looked in the case and immediately pointed out *her* ring, the one with three diamonds in a 1920s setting. But she wanted nothing to do with trying it on again. One of the ladies handed me the ring, and I slipped it on Dahlynn's protesting finger, and simply told the salesladies, "We'll take it!" I don't remember exactly what else I said—Dahlynn insists that I said nothing else—but I knew I got it right when the confusion on my future wife's face turned to a great big smile that quickly melted into tears of joy. Even the salesladies became misty-eyed.

One of the salesladies, knowing that Dahlynn and I were coauthors for Chicken Soup for the Soul books, blurted out, "Oh, that's the perfect Chicken Soup story!" And so it was, although it took me nearly six years to write it. Oh, yes, I did get down on my knee some time later and formally asked Dahlynn to marry me—and she said yes.

Ken McKowen

"I'm engaged! Look! I have Bling."

Reprinted by permission of Stephanie Piro. © 2006 Stephanie Piro.

Now, That's Love

*We are each of us angels with only one wing,
and we can fly only by embracing each other.*

Luciano de Cresendo

I was going through a very difficult time in my life. Without any warning at all, my father, to whom I was very close, died of a massive heart attack. He was here one day and gone the next. He was far too young to die. There wasn't even time to say good-bye to him. How could I explain this to my three very young sons and help them deal with his death when I didn't understand it myself? And how could I remain the happy, cheerful, and patient mother they deserved and needed when I was so sad that I almost could not get out of bed each morning?

Although my husband, Frank, was wrapped in grief too, he knew he needed to do something to help me. So, without saying a word, he decided to take charge. It was a Thursday morning, and Frank had already left for work. I sent the two older boys off to school, and I had just returned from dropping the youngest one off at preschool.

Something wasn't right, because when I returned home, Frank's car was back in the driveway. *Why is he home?* I called to him when I entered the house. He was standing in the bedroom with a suitcase in his hand. Another suitcase was by the door. *Oh great, this is the last straw! He is leaving me! But wait, what is he saying?*

He said, "The boys are taken care of, the dogs are taken care of, the house is taken care of. I have made all of the arrangements. You are being kidnapped. Pack this suitcase with enough clothes for four days. You'll need mostly casual clothes, but be sure to put in something dressy, too. I am all packed. We are leaving in exactly one hour, so you'd better get ready."

Both stunned and excited, I ran around like a crazy person trying to decide what to take with me. I wanted to wash my hair. No time. I wanted to do my nails. No time.

Exactly one hour later, we pulled out of the driveway. We headed north from Los Angeles. Frank remained mum. Each time we passed another city, I would think we were stopping. One time he even got off of the freeway, drove a couple of blocks and got right back on the freeway and continued north. *Where are we going? Ah, we must be going to San Francisco.* We loved San Francisco. Wrong again. We crossed over the Golden Gate Bridge and kept going north. A little while later he pulled off of the freeway into the lovely town of Sausalito. And he pulled up in front of an old Victorian bed and breakfast.

The hotel was a big restored 100-year-old house and was unbelievably beautiful. We checked in and were taken to our room. It was a wonderful room with an amazing view of the Bay and the San Francisco skyline. Waiting for us in the room were a dozen long stemmed red roses, a chilled bottle of champagne, and crystal champagne flutes.

Overwhelmed, I read the card that was attached to the

roses. It said, "Happy Anniversary. All my love forever." How could I have forgotten? It was our tenth anniversary. For once in my life I didn't know what to say. With everything else that was happening, this important fact slipped my mind. But Frank remembered and had planned for it.

For months, Frank had been working on all the arrangements for this trip. He was in charge. I hadn't a clue that he was up to something. Frank arranged for everything at home to run smoothly, so that I could just relax and enjoy myself; he did the research and found the hotel; he chose the room with the best view, and he ordered the roses and the champagne; he made all of the dinner reservations at a different restaurant each night. Everything was perfect. I followed along enjoying the moment. It was just what I needed. We had the most wonderful four-day weekend. It was magic.

When our long weekend ended and we returned home, I was in much better spirits. I still missed my father terribly, but I was able to smile again. Then I started to laugh again. The light came back into my life. Grieving is a process that both Frank and I needed to go through; but what a kind, generous, and loving thing Frank did for me to help me get through that process. Now, that's love.

Barbara LoMonaco

Till Death Do Us Part—Again!

The finest emotion of which we are capable is the mystic emotion.

Albert Einstein

Walking past the gold-framed mirror, I caught just a glimpse out of the corner of my eye of the young woman whose husband had just died. My heart broke for her. I knew how deeply she loved her husband and wondered how in the world she would be able to go on without him. How could she stand it? It was far more than I could ever handle. Her pain must be unbearable! In total shock, I suddenly realized the young woman in the mirror was me!

How could I possibly go on without Steve? The world suddenly seemed huge and unfriendly. I felt so utterly lost and alone. There was absolutely no doubt in my mind that Steve was in heaven. I was thrilled for him to be free at last. Never in my life had I witnessed anyone suffer so much for so long—more than four years, with over forty hospital stays. The majority of his illnesses were life-and-death situations. One instance was when Steve "died." He was brought back to life and placed on life support for over a month. Normal life handed us one trauma after another, with no breathers in between.

My heart was also overflowing with precious memories. Steve had won my heart when we were only fifteen years old. Neither of us had ever dated one person steadily. We fell in love right from the beginning. Others thought we were too serious at such a young age. Once someone almost pressured me to break up with Steve. When I tried, he became distraught. I heard a voice say, "He's going to need you." From that moment on, I never had any more doubts.

One month after graduating high school, we married because we couldn't wait to start our life together. Since that time, we have been best friends, lovers, business partners, and parents of four children. Our home filled with music as Steve played his guitar and wrote love songs to me, even after seventeen years of marriage. I felt like the most loved woman alive.

We survived his brother's suicide, fought side by side through challenging financial battles, built a business together, lost it, and watched as our home burned. We shared the births and joy of four children. Steve loved life and made sure everyone else did, too. We took spur-of-the-moment road trips and celebrated large and small occasions.

Whatever life handed us, we faced it as a team—especially Steve's mysterious illness that seemed to attack all parts of his body. About the time the doctors decided lupus was the culprit, we discovered the severe damage to his heart was irreparable. He didn't have long to live.

About six months before he died, Steve said he needed to tell me something really important, but just couldn't yet. He tried several times before he was actually able to tell me that he wanted me to marry again after he died. He knew someday I would find a really good man to love me and our kids. I immediately changed the subject. It was the last thing I wanted to hear. I wanted to enjoy every moment we were given, never knowing if it would be our last together.

No matter how prepared I thought I was for his passing, when he died I felt like half of me had been cut away without any anesthesia. I was left with a deep bleeding wound where Steve once occupied. The grief and loneliness often threatened to drown me, but I always knew God was with me. I moved forward for our children's sakes.

As the gut-wrenching grief lessened, I realized I was only thirty-seven years old, and with my genetics I'd probably live to be 103! I missed my marriage to Steve. I longed to share life with someone again. I told God that if he wanted me to, I would remain single the rest of my life. But if he found someone for me to marry, he was going to have to put the one he chose right in front of me.

Not too long after that prayer, Dwight walked into my Sunday school class and into my life. I immediately recognized his pain: grief. He was hurting deeply from a failed marriage and was rearing two children by himself. I saw the depth of Dwight's compassion and goodness; my spirit leaped within me. I didn't realize it until later, but I believe God was letting me know this was the man he'd picked out for me. As practically the only two singles in our church, everyone enjoyed watching our romance grow.

When Steve died, I felt like an eighty-five-year-old. We had lived through so much, it seemed like several lifetimes. But as Dwight and I fell in love, I began to feel young again. At the same time I was shocked to discover that I could love someone else. It didn't take away my love for Steve. Instead, I had even more love to give Dwight and his kids. I'm grateful Steve told me I would marry again. It was as if he knew.

Not long after our wedding, Dwight and I traveled out of state on our first trip together to visit his dad. That night as we slept in the guest bedroom, I dreamed Steve walked in. It was wonderful to see him again! He looked completely healthy! He wanted to see how I was doing and to meet Dwight. He told me what a really great guy Dwight was and that he was very happy for me. Then he left, leaving me filled with peace and an even greater love and appreciation for my new husband.

The next morning as we drove back home, Dwight casually reported that he had dreamed about Steve the night before.

"Oh, really?" My mouth dropped open. Since I hadn't told him of my dream, I couldn't wait to hear what he said next.

"Yeah. It was really nice. It seemed he just wanted to meet me. Steve told me he was very happy for both of us and then left."

I never believed that the deep pain of my grief could heal and that I would be given another chance to be blessed by love. Life is full of trials and joys. You never know what's up ahead! Dwight and I are having fun discovering it together.

Eva Juliuson

Some Assembly Required

"Do you, Paul, take Deborah to be your lawfully wedded wife, to have and to hold, from this day forward, for better, for worse, for richer, for poorer, in sickness or in health, to love and to cherish till death do you part?" asks Reverend James.

In front of a multitude of family and friends, I reply, "I do!"

Our love endures the test of time, and we remain as dedicated to each other today as we did twelve years ago. However, when Reverend James read those solemn wedding vows, I do not recall him mentioning anything about my obligation to assemble those lovely knickknacks my wife loves to buy. Yet, my moral obligation binds me to endure enormous hardship and suffer tremendous stress to carefully assemble these beautiful works of art for her visual pleasure.

My wife, bless her heart, loves to adorn our humble home with many different and unique knickknacks in a variety of styles and sizes. She eagerly pores through scores of home decorating catalogs as she seeks out the perfect item for each square inch of wall, shelf, floor, and table space. Her current theme is nautical, and our dining room, living room, and kitchen are reminiscent of an old fisherman's dock house.

Alas, there is some available space in our living area that may accommodate a small stool that catches the eyes of my wife. I note the odd expressions of awe and joy as she reads over the wordy description. Subsequently, she flips the thick catalog around and shows me a picture of her desired object. I give an approving nod and feign interest, as if that would sway her decision either way. After some administrative work and a little bit of our hard-earned income, she orders the stool.

Segue to a country very far away from my home, where they cut, drill, paint, and lovingly package stool pieces for an arduous journey to a happy consumer. I envision a small factory where a group of workers huddle closely around a lunch table, sharing camaraderie while eating and laughing. The object of laughter is their mischievous abuse of machinery. Those happy workers are fully aware that the holes they drilled in the parts and pieces of those exquisite home decorations manufactured there will never line up and will cause customers horrendous anguish later. Adding to their mirth are those indecipherable instructions they carefully tuck into each Styrofoam travel caddy.

BAM! I hurl a screwdriver through the living room wall with a convincing thud. I hate that screwdriver and that wall needs some patching and a fresh coat of paint anyway. One page—four pictures—no words, how hard could it be? This should be no match for an experienced craftsman and stool assembler like me. Imagine my delight at the receipt of my wife's desire, the infamous unassembled nautical stool.

"*Expletive, expletive* stool," I roar.

A small threaded cylinder must fit into a small hole in a

leg of the stool. A long skinny screw should fit through a hole in the brace and thread into the small cylinder in the leg. This looks easy enough. However, I must hold the leg, small cylinder, brace, and turn a screwdriver on a long skinny screw to make this all fit together. A slight problem: I do not have enough hands to complete the first step in the assembly. Add to that, the part's holes do not line up, and nothing looks like the picture.

"Do you need any help?" my wife questions.

She already knows the answer. This would mean accepting defeat early in the game, like invoking the mercy rule in the first inning of a softball game. I realize my manhood is in jeopardy. Her help could threaten the entire male species. Those pioneering men who rolled across America in the early days and single-handedly built this great nation would roll in their graves if I allowed this travesty. Thomas Edison did not call his wife, Mary, to help him with the telephone invention. George Washington did not invoke his Martha's help when he bravely crossed the Delaware River. I maintained my composure, stepped back, and stayed cool. A woman is trying to invade the man's realm of wood and tools. No way, no how, not on my watch.

"No," I cheerfully reply.

I am a master of tools, a self-proclaimed master craftsman, and I own a myriad of tools and a garage cluttered with "stuff" to prove it. Summing up my reserve testosterone hidden deeply away and preserved for only these rare occasions, I protrude my chest and move on. During another attempt to join parts, suddenly and without warning, all the parts tumble to the floor. To add insult to injury, as the stool's leg is falling, it tips the bowls filled with carefully separated screws, causing them to spew haphazardly into the thick pile of the living room carpet.

A cordless drill, assorted drill bits, belt sander, hammer,

six screwdrivers, sandpaper, tubs of wood glue, my secret box of extra screws and nails, wood clamps, a Black & Decker Workmate, and a jigsaw haphazardly strewn about the living room stands like monuments, a testament to my woodworking prowess. Finally, the stool with the brush-painted seagulls, ocean waves slapping a treacherous seashore, and lighthouse stands magnificently in my living room. My wife beams with pride at my accomplishments and her good taste. So far, to my delight, she has not said anything about the hole in the living room wall.

A leafy plant will decorate the new stool. Its monstrous clay pot and hefty leaves and cumbersome vines lower to within inches of the fruit of my labor—I wince. Those glued joints may not be totally set. I agonize over each passing inch as the weight of 1,000 elephants loom dangerously close to the conglomeration of wood, glue, and odd screws. After what seems like an eternity, the story ends happily. A picturesque potted plant has found a new home atop this nautical perch. Chest pushed out, I am a man among men, a caring and nurturing caregiver to my dear wife, and a builder of finely crafted furniture.

Time to close up shop. Feeling good about myself, I begin to store my tools in their perspective nesting grounds deep within the bowels of my garage sanctuary. Suddenly and without warning, a chill shoots up my spine. A fear grips me so intensely that I am frozen in my tracks, unable to move, even utter a sound. My hair feels as if it is standing on end.

"If you have time, can you put this lighthouse tissue holder together for me?" my wife asks.

Paul James

Waiting on Wyoming

Friends for more than six years, Dave and I finally saw what all of our family and friends also knew: we were a great fit as a couple. We had consoled and supported each other through numerous failed relationships, and now we were happily settled into married life.

In October 2003, married for almost two years, everything in my life seemed to be falling into place. Dave and I welcomed our first son, Mason, into our family.

Then on November 4, 2003, Dave received "the call." Dave is a longtime member of the California Army National Guard; he was being deployed to Iraq. I don't remember any other time that I felt such a horrible mix of emotions, but at the same time I was as proud as I had ever felt because he was willing to serve our country. It was clear that Dave would go to Iraq, I would stay home and take care of Mason, and we would find a way to get through this very difficult time.

The first five months of the eighteen-month deployment, Dave was stateside for training. Mason and I stayed in California, while Dave trained in cold, snowy Ft. Lewis, Washington. While we adjusted to the separation, I tried to come up with something to help count down the days for Dave's safe return home. I planned to send Dave lots of cards and letters, but I wanted a fun and meaningful way to help him gauge how soon he would be returning to his family in California.

Some families make a paper chain, with each link representing a day, and then decorate with the completed chain for the welcome home. Others mark X's on the calendar squares to see the days go by. I wanted something more interactive, something we could do together.

Standing in line at the post office to buy postage stamps, I found my idea: postcards of the fifty United States. *This is perfect* I thought. There are fifty states and just about that many weeks in a year. One postcard mailed the same day each week will arrive on a regular basis, giving Dave something to look forward to. With a personal, loving note from me on one side, and a visual reminder of each state that he is representing and protecting while in Iraq, this was my answer.

When I sent Dave the first card, Alabama, I wrote about how I wanted to visit Alabama with him when he returned home. I referenced something little known about the state and reminded him he had only forty-nine more weeks to go. The next week he received Alaska, then Arkansas, and after that Arizona. On every card I wrote about something we could do or see when we would visit that state. I also added a reminder about how appreciative we Americans are, in every state, for every one of our men and women serving to keep us safe back home.

I can't recall exactly when, but not long after the alphabetical pattern had become clear, I received an e-mail that simply read, "Waiting on Wyoming. I love you. Love, Dave." It worked! Dave looked forward to mail call and always looked for his next postcard. I sent other cards and letters, but it was the postcards of the United States that decorated the inside of his tent. While other families were marking off days on a calendar, Dave was marking off states with a black marker on a small map. On that map was a very clear focal point, a big red heart circling the state of Wyoming with the words "waiting on Wyoming" written in small letters.

On February 1, 2005, Dave and his unit were frantically packing and preparing for the long trip home. Nobody was thinking about mail and was far less concerned about letters and more concerned with getting all the details signed off so they could process out of Iraq and come back into America. As Dave hurried to take care of his administrative business, he slipped away to the mail tent. He found the last bundle of mail he would receive in Iraq. Flipping through several pieces of mail, he found it, like a bright spot of sunshine, the colorful little card reading in big letters across the front, "WYOMING." With a big smile and a sense of pride, he put the card into his pocket and finished his work.

More than a year later, while unpacking a box he had shipped home, he came across the rubber-banded bundle of postcards. He pulled them out and shared with me what they meant to him. He told me that not only did he enjoy the game, but more important, he felt the sense of pride and responsibility a soldier feels with regard to protecting our country. He said he just couldn't come home without Wyoming. Knowing he had all fifty of his states, he was ready to return home to his happily married family life.

Kathleen Partak

Tough Decisions

Hearing is one of the body's five senses. But listening is an art.

Frank Tyger

My husband, Ray, looked at his watch and pushed his chair back from the kitchen table. "It's time to go see Mom," he said.

"I'm ready." I picked up the hefty shoulder bag in which I carry half the world. "Maybe when we get there we should ask about moving Hazel to the Health Center, where she can get twenty-four-hour care."

Ray set his jaw. He had done this only a few times during our four years of marriage. "I don't think so. She can still manage on her own. She always pays her bills."

Was that the ultimate test? Hazel lived in a wonderful assisted living center with graduated care. Clearly she, like her father and sister, had Alzheimer's. *Why wouldn't he want the best for her?* Ray was so stubborn. "Didn't you say she paid her quarterly taxes twice?" I asked, setting my purse back on the counter. "And last week she gave you an empty phone envelope to mail that she had stamped and sealed." I could be stubborn, too.

"She has a bad day once in a while." Ray began shuffling things around on the counter: a message pad, random pieces of mail, and a bowl of M&M's.

I knew I should let the matter drop. This second marriage for us both promised to be far happier than our first ones. He was obviously devastated by his mother's illness and felt he could somehow do something for her. In reality, he couldn't. I wanted to hold and comfort him, not fight with him.

Another part of me felt I must try to get Hazel assistance. Ray faithfully visited her at least once a week, but she needed help with daily routines, such as walking to meals and taking medications. I reached across the table and took his hand. "I helped her change her blouse when she spilled tea on it last Sunday," I said gently. "She had on two bras."

"That's better than no bra." I might have smiled if Ray weren't so serious and his mother's needs so great. "She gets confused sometimes," he said, taking his hand away. "That's all. You will too when you're eighty-six."

Tension filled the short distance between us. I took a sip of tea, then a deep breath. "I'm really worried about her. Her medications, her—"

"If you don't want to go with me to visit her," Ray interrupted, "just say so. I'll go alone." He pushed the M&M's aside and strode from the room.

Of course I wanted to go. My own mother had died a decade before, and Hazel was my mother now. I felt as though the ground shifted beneath me as I watched him leave, my husband, whom I loved, off to visit my mother-in-law, whom I also loved. I didn't know how to help either one.

Four hours later, Ray walked back into the house, his

face pale, his eyes worried. "I had a good talk with Mom about taking her meds. I think she'll remember," he said, not bothering with a "hello," or "sorry about this morning."

She won't remember, I wanted to say, but he'd never walked out on me before. I wasn't just worried about Hazel. I was worried about us.

"There was some bad news, though." Ray ran his hand through his hair. "Maxine captured me in the hall. You know Maxine."

I remembered Maxine well. She and Hazel were friends long before they both moved into the manor. I took Ray's hand and led him to the couch, where he allowed the weight of his shoulder to press against mine as we sat side by side. *So much nicer than our standoff this morning,* I thought.

"Maxine said Mom's been missing breakfast a lot lately. And she can't converse with the other people at the table when she does come. Maxine thinks she belongs in the Health Center."

Kudos to Maxine, I thought, relief flooding my chest. *If the idea sounded better coming from her than me, that was fine.*

"But I don't agree," Ray said. "Somebody could check that she's awake and ready."

I let go of his hand and moved to the other side of the couch, nabbing a throw pillow to cuddle in my lap as I did my stuffed animals when I was a child. I couldn't support him in his fantasy that his mother could still live independently. It wasn't fair to Hazel. So evidently we would have either verbal warfare or hostile silence.

That night in bed, Ray faced the wall. His body was rigid when I touched his shoulder, and he turned away from my attempt at a kiss.

I'd been reading about Alzheimer's online, trying to come up with something that might help us get through this time, individually and as a couple. I knew that those who carried the emotional caregiving often struggled more than the physical caregivers, but I didn't know what to do about it. My mind wandered between worrying about Ray, worrying about Hazel, and worrying about our marriage. I saw an endless string of arguments ahead of us.

I was right. Every week before Ray and I visited Hazel, he had a headache, and when he got home it was worse. Those days his personality changed. Usually a kind, complimentary person, he found fault with everything I did. I tried to tease him. "Amazing how incompetent I can become in just one day," I said. But it wasn't funny.

Meanwhile, I saw Hazel's health further deteriorate. She was thin, anxious, and unable to track simple conversations. She simply couldn't manage living alone. Still, Ray resisted moving her.

One evening as Ray and I watched the news, Michele, Ray's oldest daughter, called, almost crying. She and her sister Tracy took a precious day on spring break to load up all their children and visit Grandma. Only Grandma, who at one time remembered every great-grandchild's birthday with a card and gift, couldn't remember any of their names.

Tracy called us, too, to share her grief. "She asks the same questions over and over. She's there, but she's not. She's not the same person she used to be."

Ray twisted and untwisted the phone cord as he sought to comfort his daughters. My heart ached for us all.

The next morning, while I fixed breakfast, Ray paced the kitchen floor. "Michele and Tracy were so shook up," he said. "It is scary to see Mom that way. Maybe . . . I'm not sure . . . if I just . . ." His voice trailed off.

"You can't do it all, sweetie," I said. "Nobody can." Then an idea struck me. "What if we got your mother a companion? Someone to help her out with the things she can't manage. The manor must have a list of experienced people we could consider."

Ray stopped his pacing. "I feel like I should be able to take care of things for her."

I walked to him, put my arms around him, and kissed his cheek. "You can't do it all," I said again. "You're a wonderful son, but you can't. If you want me to, I'll make the calls and arrange for someone."

Ray sighed so deeply that his body shuddered. "See if you can find somebody to spend a part of each day with her. That would be great. And maybe—maybe after she's spent some time with Mom, she can advise us if it's time for the Alzheimer's unit."

As we lay in bed that night, this time holding each other, Ray thanked me for helping him see a different way to take care of his mother. I thanked him for being open to what I said. I knew we would face some hard, sad times as his mother progressed through Alzheimer's. But I knew, too, that we would find a way to talk and to listen.

Samantha Waltz

Crown of Commitment

I felt it shelter to speak to you.

Emily Dickinson

I sigh with delight as memories of my wedding day dance in my head. The guests waited with anticipation. Their whispers mixed with a soft and delicate melody coming from the piano. My bridegroom, Gene, waited for me at the altar. The music changed—my sign to begin my walk down the aisle.

"Are you ready?" whispered my dad hesitantly.

I nodded and put my trembling arm through his. We proceeded down the aisle with marked steps to the tune of royal and elegant trumpets echoing loudly through the church. My steps were slow, but my heart beat fast. The artistic arrangements of fresh flowers along the sides laced an invisible canopy of soft fragrances. The sun beaming through the huge stained-glass windows painted colorful reflections on the marble floor.

Dressed in pure white, I joined my prince. "For better or for worse . . ."

Those words held a distant concept back then, and my heart lit up with dreams of the "better." But nine years later, my world darkened with the reality of the "worse," and those words echoed with a sobering truth.

"What I can see is a clear deterioration of the retina," said the ophthalmologist. "You need to prepare." He paused, then he added with coldness, "No one knows how long you'll have your sight."

He's wrong. It won't happen. I can see just fine, I reasoned.

Each day became a test of the amount of sight I still had left. One week I could see the furniture around me, the next I could perceive only portions of some items.

It's okay, I can still see what's important—my three little boys' faces, were my comforting thoughts.

But the months that followed ushered the dreaded blindness. Out of habit, I felt for the light switch in our bathroom, I flipped it on, but—the darkness remained. My body shook with terror. Holding on to the cold slick countertop, I looked toward the mirror and saw a dreary-gray nothing. In desperation, I felt the urge to scratch through the glass into the darkness to find even a slight glimpse of my reflection. Instead, I found the ugliness of my black world. "Why me, Lord!" I angrily shouted.

Gene came into the bathroom and startled me. "Are you okay?" he asked.

"No, I'm not!" I screamed as I pounded on the countertop.

Help me, God. Help me to face him, face my children, and face myself, my heart begged.

He held my hand and whispered, "It'll be okay." He gently brushed some hair strands from my face.

Years swept by, turning the pages of our life together. Some were stained with the pain of losing our youngest son, others wrinkled with adjustments to unexpected financial setbacks, and the pages of my blindness were carefully taped together. But each page, framed with a rainbow of colors, reflects God's sustaining power.

Although unable to see my own reflection, I see God's image in the mirror of our marriage. The faint but sweet aroma of Gene's cologne surrounds me with delight as he holds my hand and prays for my day before he leaves for work.

On other occasions as we drive out of our neighborhood, Gene remarks, with sweetness in his voice, "My baby sure looks beautiful." I smile with gratitude as he takes my hand, brings it to his lips, and places a gentle kiss.

When I comment, "It sure is chilly in this restaurant, isn't it?" I feel a light sweater around me. Gene would quickly slip away and retrieve it from the car. He drapes it around me and deposits a kiss on my cheek.

Walking hand in hand among the racks of clothes in a department store, Gene says softly, "Okay, let's see what looks perfect on my beautiful girl."

I hurriedly try on the clothes he picks out and model them for him. "What do you think? Do you like this one better?" I ask, waiting to hear his opinion.

"They all look great on you, especially that red one with your black hair!" he comments. "We'll take them all."

Lying next to my sleeping husband, I stretch my hand to find his strong arm. In the stillness of the night, my thoughts race. Although my eyes have lost their function to see, I can still cry. Tears stream down my cheeks as the well of gratitude within me overflow. Listening to the sound of Gene's rhythmic breathing, I sigh with admiration for the man who saw beyond the ugliness of my blindness, and with his love, turned me into a queen.

As I sit across from him on our patio, my thoughts wander. *How I wish I could return what he has given me—his unconditional love. How I long to say, "Don't worry, honey. Stay home and rest. I'll take care of those errands." Or "How about if I read something to you for a change?"* But this will not happen.

After reading some chapters, he takes a break. I ask, "Do you sometimes wish you were married to someone who could see?" I've never asked this before, but I continue. "Then you wouldn't need to do so much. Tell me the truth." I hold my breath waiting for his answer.

"The truth is you probably do much more for me than I ever do for you," he says. "We make a good team just the way we are, and we'll make it to the end. We have God as our coach."

In silence, I ponder his last sentence. It reveals an important truth. God is our coach, and he calls the plays: to submit and to love.

With my eyes fixed on God, I submitted to Gene's love. And as he followed God's instructions, he handed me the treasure of his love. And his devotion shines as jewels that sparkle on the crown of his commitment.

Janet Perez Eckles

I Love You

I am so proud to say whom I fell in love with—and vowed
  to love to the very end—
Is still not only my lover, but also my best friend.
Our love story began in the small town of Sullivan—April
  15 was our first date.
When this soft-spoken guy with big beautiful brown eyes
  asked me to skate.
"I do not skate very well as you can see . . .
"But the next couple-skate, I would like you to skate with
  me."
Well . . . to say the least, he had my heart.
This was twenty years ago, when at ages fourteen and fif-
  teen our love story would start.
We stayed sweethearts at Webster County High, became
  engaged at Murray State.
Now celebrating eighteen years of marriage, May 16 being
  our wedding date.
Married to this man has been *wonderful*—but not without
  some doubts.
Without his support—as far as children—we would have
  had to learn to do without.
Doctors said that maybe it just wasn't meant to be.

However, they just didn't know how much Terry loved me.

At this time in our marriage I tried to push him away.

I was the reason why we could not have children, so with me he should not have to stay!

He replied, "We both want children—you know this is true.

"But we can adopt children, but I can't adopt you!

"If I was the one with the problem, you would not leave me. So we'll get through this together—it will be okay, you'll see!"

For two years I leaned on him to be strong, and he would not let me down.

Until June 7 our miracle arrived—Savannah Ashley Brown.

But our family would not end here, I am happy to say.

When three years later, Cameron Michael came our way!

As we tuck our children into bed, I realize doctors are smart.

However, they did underestimate the power of the heart.

Whether it's my daughter, who has her dad's big beautiful brown eyes, or my son, who has his dad's dimpled grin,

Every time I look at them, I fall in love again.

With that same big brown-eyed boy who did not know how to skate,

But knew just how to glide into my heart and make my life great!

Each night as I cuddle with this man so loving and fun,

I think that it is just a shame that God did not make more than one!

Stephanie Ray Brown

First Kiss

'Twas not my lips you kissed but my soul.

Judy Garland

By the time Louie and I had known each other a few weeks, I hoped he would try to kiss me, but he never did. And by the time that we had known each other a couple of months, I began to wonder what was wrong with me. Everything about Louie attracted me: his good looks, his sense of humor, his kindness, and his decency. He was so likeable that I had this incredible urge to grab him and hug him to death. I did not know that he felt the same way about me.

In my past, I would have received a first-place award for choosing unsafe men to marry. When I first met Louie, I was running from an abusive marriage. I was divorced and determined to stay that way. I had three young daughters, and I never had any idea what to look for in a man, so why start now.

Louie was everything I ever dreamed of. He was safe, protective, funny, even silly and kind; he was big and strong, with an irresistible Tennessee mountain twang and a shy respectfulness that absolutely delighted me. We shared a love of books. He seemed so taken with me, and when I discovered that I could make him laugh, I was enchanted! However, Louie's love for my children really stole my heart. They absolutely worshipped him. Louie's affection and kindness were new to my wounded little girls, and I loved him for the joy that he put on their faces.

Jenny, particularly vulnerable to the cruelty of my ex-husband, was an easy target. She suffered hearing impairment and juvenile rheumatoid arthritis. Like a whipped dog, Jenny desperately needed sensitive, caring affection. She adored Louie, but she was also filled with uncertainty and fear.

One night as we watched television together, Louie was sitting on the floor, with my youngest child sprawled next to him. I watched Jenny as she began a kind of hopeless ballet. It was obvious that she was attempting to sit on his lap, but her fear of rejection made her unable to negotiate the move. Oh, how I wanted Louie to notice how badly she needed him to hold her.

Jenny would back up to his lap, and do a little bob and wag, never quite making contact. I sent a silent prayer heavenward. *Oh, please, Lord, don't let him reject her.* Finally, I beckoned Jenny over to me, and I whispered into her ear.

"Jenny, take a chance. Sometimes we need to take the risk of getting hurt in order to find out if someone is safe to love." Jenny nodded her head, and she squared her shoulders. She walked over to Louie, continuing to bob and wag. I held my breath as Louie suddenly noticed her little recital. Reaching out, he swooped her into his arms and hugged her close. Jenny burst into sobs, her face contorted with relief.

Silently, Louie held her as he patted her back. "There, there," he whispered.

I think that's when I fell in love with him. I never knew anyone as compassionate and understanding. Right then and there, I made up my mind that he would not leave my house without being kissed. I didn't know how to negotiate that, but I felt it would happen. I put the children to bed by nine o'clock, and Louie and I sat on the couch and talked until midnight. I told him all about Jenny, and how much courage it took for her to risk his rejection.

"I wouldn't have rejected that little girl to save my life," he said after some thought. "How could anyone resist that sweet face? When Jenny burst into tears, I thought I was going to break down in sobs myself."

I found his simple honesty amazing. I looked into his eyes, and I wondered what wonderful planet this man had come from. Our eyes met and held, and I knew he wanted to kiss me, but he never made a move. We talked long into the night, and I could feel myself sweetly falling deeper in love.

It was early morning when Louie stood up. As I walked him to the door, he reached out to give me a hug—and a brotherly kiss on the cheek. That's when I reached up and turned his face toward mine. I kissed him softly on the lips.

Something like lightening shot through me. A powerful sweetness and a warm blaze of fire tore through my heart. I could feel his gentle fingers brushing through my hair. I thought I would faint. It was over too quickly, then he left. I don't think I breathed again for the rest of night. I was certain he would never come back. It was just too powerful.

Much to my joy, Louie did return. Our love blossomed and grew into a long and happy marriage. My amazement at the love I feel for this man and his love for me never ceases—I never regretted giving him that first kiss.

Jaye Lewis

"Even if it were you proposing to me,
you would tell everyone I proposed to you."

Beware the Setting Sun

Walking with a friend in the dark is better than walking alone in the light

Helen Keller

Scared to death adequately describes how I felt in the theater that night when the young American man on the screen walked across the moors in the light of a full moon and was bitten by a werewolf. It was so real that I burrowed into my husband's lap, buried my head beneath his shirt, and prayed that awful creature on the screen would disappear.

Irrational? Perhaps. But we all get a little scared from time to time. And when frightened, a person will run to the safest place he or she knows. For me, it is my husband's arms.

"You really know how to pick a movie, don't you?" Tom teased as I peeked up at him with wide, terrified eyes. Watching scary movies had never bothered me before, but when the wolf in this movie howled, all sense of make-believe was lost.

We were celebrating a special night—our fifth wedding

anniversary. Wanting to splurge for a change, I found a sitter so we could go out for a lengthy dinner and a movie.

I love going to the movies. But the movie we saw that night maimed me for life. To this day, every time I empty my pockets, I expect to find a half-chewed human finger, just as the man in the movie did! Honestly, sitting through that movie was the single most terrifyingly scary thing I ever endured. It scared me so thoroughly that I'm still afraid of the dark.

Back in the '80s, we lived and reared our daughters in a tiny cabin by a mud hole of a lake, and my closest relative was more than an hour away. The area wasn't remote, but it was dark and overgrown. Our neighbors reassured me there was nothing to be frightened of. They said their dogs would protect us. I did not feel safer when I found out their dogs were part wolf. As I recall, it was the same day Tom was bumped to the afternoon shift at work.

Each day I kissed my husband good-bye, then watched with dread as the sun set. Because our half-acre lot was secluded, we didn't need to hang curtains on the back windows. But when the sun went down and I stared at those dark windows, my mind conjured up all sorts of nightmarish creatures that might be prowling around. The next day when Tom pulled out of the driveway, I pinned beach towels over the windows. As long as I couldn't see the darkness, I didn't think about werewolves and other such scary creatures.

The next weekend Tom got out the tape measure.

"What are you doing, Daddy?" Our two-year-old daughter, Alissa, asked.

"I was thinking maybe we could get some blinds for the living room," he said as our four-year-old daughter, April, raced to hold the tape measure in place.

I poked my head out of the kitchen doorway and quickly agreed. "I think that's a great idea!" I said, smiling as he tickled our youngsters with the tip of the tape measure until they were rolling on the floor in fits of laughter.

"Or curtains," I added as I wiped my soapy hands on a dish towel.

He smiled. "Better than beach towels?"

I smiled back, embarrassed. "Much better."

Once the curtains were in place, I breathed easier from Saturday to Thursday. But when Friday evening rolled around, I had to bite the bullet—and I don't mean silver bullet. Friday evenings were reserved for grocery shopping. Pre-werewolf movie, I enjoyed Friday nights. Post-werewolf movie, however, and my newly developed phobia of the dark, I no longer shuffled down the grocery aisles checking out everything. I booked it! I was in a race with the setting sun. I was fine in the car after dark. But getting out of the car and into the house in the dark was the hard part.

Beeping the horn to signal my arrival home would have been the easiest, but I didn't want to wake up the kids, so I refrained. Instead, I shut off the engine, left the headlights on, took a deep breath, grabbed my purse, jumped out, and raced down the sidewalk, then up the three porch steps. From there I unlocked the door and quickly slipped inside. Once inside, I breathed a sigh of relief and then enlisted Tom's help for the remainder of the groceries. I'm ashamed to admit that one time when I arrived home and Tom was sleeping with the children on his lap, I didn't have the nerve to go back outside alone. Instead, I left a bag—filled with perishables—in the car overnight. I cried the next morning when I had to toss a week's worth of groceries into the trash, groceries we could not afford to replace.

The day after my crying jag, Tom cut out the bushes that circled the house near the driveway, as well as the bushes along the front fence. Then he hooked up a yard light that shined a beam of clear bright light in both directions: down the driveway all the way to the street as well as into the backyard.

Not long after the light was in place and sucking up loads of electricity, a TV special titled *The Making of the Movie An American Werewolf in London* aired. Tom said if I watched it I'd realize how fake it all was, and maybe I'd be able to accept it as nothing more than a movie and thereby get over my fear.

I was skeptical at first, but he was right. I was fine until the wolf howled and transported me back in time to a dark theater, and all I could think of was clawing my way under his shirt again.

Today, twenty years later, I'm over it . . . almost. Of course, it might have something to do with the fact that Tom makes sure the yard light remains on all night and has no objection to the miniature white lights I string around the backyard year round—meter be damned.

Everyone in every marriage has to learn and grow together as well as individually. A couple of the most important things I've learned over the years include: Never walk on the moors at night—doesn't matter if you're with your best friend or not—and all fear dissolves into nothingness when Tom slips his hand into mine.

He is my safety zone and I am his. Alone we do not have the same strength. But together, we become the safe place we both seek. Nothing is more important to our marriage or the love we feel for each other than the simple act of being there—no questions asked. Judgment, ridicule, and abandonment do not exist in our "safety zone."

When he holds me in his arms and comforts me, I know the deepest kind of love—the unconditional kind. And though Tom is the strong, silent type and doesn't often speak of such things, I know he feels it, too.

Helen Kay Polaski

From Paw to Hand

If I weren't such a hopeful woman, I might have broken the deal: My fiancé didn't like cats. The day I met my future husband, he asked me whom I lived with.

"Mikey," I said.

"Who is Mikey?"

"He's solid blue-gray, the color of a seal, with eyes of an owl. He weighs about six pounds and suffers from an extreme case of colitis. And his breath—his breath smells like an elixir of glue and tuna. But he's beautiful. He's my best friend."

Just the thought of Mikey filled my heart with love. He was a precious treasure who kept me company through the hardest of times. Yes, I had people in my life who stayed by my side through years of extreme physical illness and the accompanying depression, but humans—even the best intended—come with judgments, well-meaning advice, and their own particular views. Mikey, on the other hand, wasted none of our precious time together assigning guilt or judgment. He knew that my abrupt departure of my well-paying job was because I was in too much pain to continue in it. Unlike my parents, his first thought wasn't how I was to pay the bills. His only statement on the matter was a deeply satisfied purr.

As the weeks following my resignation passed, my illness was misdiagnosed as mononucleosis and an array of
lesser viruses. Each day I had new symptoms: throbbing
muscles and body pain so overwhelming a sheet was too
heavy on my skin. I'd wake every few hours bathed in
cold sweat, but burning up with fever. I had no appetite,
no thoughts, no wants and needs. I barely existed—weeks
slipped into months until there was no way left to support
myself. My company had wonderfully sponsored me for a
few months, hoping I'd return, but I knew it would never
happen. The day I called the president of the company to
tell her I wouldn't be back, I felt sad. I loved my job.

I slid back into bed and pulled Mikey close. He, too, felt
warm. It struck me that he pretty much mirrored my
activity each day. When I was in bed, he was in bed. If I got
up to try to eat, Mikey would softly pad over to his bowls
to take a few licks of water and a mouthful of kibble. If I
headed to the bathroom, so did Mikey. He was my
shadow. An overt example of loyalty and selflessness,
Mikey put his head on the pillow next to mine. I'd whisper to him my hopes: getting well, meeting someone special for the both of us, writing again.

Within six months, my physical condition had
worsened. I moved from New Hampshire to North
Carolina to stay with my sister, a nurse with ties to a good
medical system. I found new doctors and finally made
some progress. One doctor in particular visited me during
an especially bad hospital stay. I existed on high doses of
pain medication administered by IV and was drifting in
and out of consciousness. I woke to see the closest replica
of Santa Claus I'd ever seen standing over my bed: a
white-haired man with that distinctive twinkle in his eye.
After speaking with me for an hour, he had an idea. He ran
some tests, and I finally received a diagnosis: a rare

airborne virus. The effects could stay a couple weeks or year upon year. Feeling better with a diagnosis and a regimen, I returned home to Mikey, who was faring much worse. He had developed an extreme case of colitis. Whereas I had finally found a doctor who provided me with some hope, I couldn't find a vet who could offer hope for Mikey. He ate less and less, began losing his fur, and had terrible bouts several times a day. I constantly cleaned up after him as only a loving "mother" could. Everyone else turned their noses, thinking he was disgusting and should be put down.

The day I met Andrew, my future husband, I had a lot on my mind. I had moved out of my sister's house into a new apartment. I was still pretty sick and took lots of medications. I had no idea how I was going to move. I had no idea how the new roommate would adjust to Mikey or how I could keep his health problem a secret. Then Andrew came into my life like an angel—out of the blue and ready to help. He lifted the boxes I couldn't and took me to the store for notions. While I enjoyed my new relationship, I wasn't faring so well in my new apartment. Mikey got worse, and keeping his accidents hidden proved difficult. Like a break in the clouds, Andrew's roommate moved out. Though we hadn't known each other long, we took the chance and decided to live together. Once again, Andrew helped me pack and move my boxes. He was less than thrilled about the cat. He was worried that Mikey would damage his apartment. Plus, he never liked cats—never saw their necessity. A dog, you could play Frisbee with. But he fell in love with me, and begrudgingly took Mikey home.

Days passed, and Mikey grew worse. He couldn't keep anything down and he was getting so tiny. After multiple consultations, I realized I was hurting him by keeping him alive. That concept was impossible for me to wrestle with.

He purred nonstop. If awake, he was in my lap or lying next to me, nuzzling my face. Andrew would shake his head and offer some hard advice. He suggested dropping him at the Humane Society if I didn't want to make the decision. I shook my head, but I knew what needed to be done.

I called the vet, knowing it was time for Mikey to finally have peace. The vet gave me the name of a pet funeral home he thought might help in my grieving process. I called and booked the services I needed and spent the night before alone with Mikey. I held him, weeping and kissing his face. Andrew was so worried he called my mother for advice. She told him to light a candle, get me some warm milk, and put me to bed. He took care of me gently, and put Mikey right beside me for the last time.

The next morning dawned bright, and as I opened my eyes, I resolved to face the day. I looked at Mikey sleeping and wondered if he knew. If he did, he was at peace. Andrew and I dressed silently. As we walked to the car, I noticed he had prepared a box with a blanket. We hardly exchanged a word in the car, but kept looking at the blue-gray cat in my lap. The veterinary appointment went quickly. The vet was so kind. He let us both be with Mikey during the process: I held his head and stroked his face and Andrew held his body until we knew he was gone. I turned to Andrew, buried my face in his shirt, and collapsed into terrible, howling grief. I felt such a mixture of emotions. Inside I even felt a little angry, thinking to myself maybe this is was what Andrew wanted all along. I looked up at his face, and what I saw surprised me. Tears, just like mine, were rolling down his face. The vet placed Mikey in the box, and we carried him to the car. At the funeral home we said good-bye to Mikey, though we knew his life was already gone. His face, once so full of love, was blank. But I still cherished his body and said a proper good-bye. The next day we returned for his ashes.

Andrew and I recently decided to marry and return to my home in New England. I wanted to take Mikey with me. *With us.* Andrew told me as we drove home with his ashes that he held a deep gratitude and respect for the cat who had kept me loved and safe until we had found each other. The baton had been passed from paw to hand. I knew I had found the right man, and knew then what has become the truth today: Cats would always be welcome in our home. They're loved as genuinely and deeply by Andrew as they are by me.

Heather Cook Lindsay

"Real comfort comes from those who know us best!"

Reprinted by permission of Stephanie Piro. © 2007 Stephanie Piro.

5

THROUGH THE
EYES OF A CHILD

In youth we learn; in age we understand.

Marie Ebner-Eschenbach

A Kind of, Almost, Sort of First Date

At the age of ten, my younger son went on a "kind of, sort of, almost date." At least that's how he described it to me. One Saturday, we discovered an extra ticket for Sunday's Chicago Cubs baseball game, and my mother suggested that my son Bobby invite a particular friend whom he talked about a lot. A *female* friend!

"Do you think I should do what Grandma said?" Bobby asked me uncertainly.

"That's up to you," I replied.

"Okay, I'll think about it," he said. A full thirty seconds later, he was on the phone with his friend.

"What did Beth say?" I asked, after he hung up.

"She had a terrible time making up her mind."

"Why?" I asked.

"'Cause she told me she'd like to spend the afternoon with me, but she hates baseball!"

"What did she finally decide?"

"That I'm worth suffering for!"

Bobby had a difficult time falling asleep that night. He was more excited than I had ever seen him. But when morning came, the weather was so miserable that we weren't able to go to the baseball game after all.

He wandered around the house in a state of despair. "Beth will be so disappointed," he repeated over and over again, not willing to admit how disappointed he was. I noticed he was on the verge of tears.

"Maybe you can still spend the afternoon together," I suggested.

"Doing what?" he asked, his mood changing instantly.

"Well, how about a movie?"

"Gee, I don't know." He hesitated. "That would be like going on a kind of . . . sort of . . . almost date."

"Why would going to a movie be any different from going to a baseball game?" I asked.

"Because you and Daddy, Steve [big brother], and Grandma were going to the game, too," he explained. "If Beth and I go to a movie, we'll be all alone."

"We can all go with you if you like," I offered, trying to help.

"No, that's okay," he quickly declared. "I'll call her to see if she wants to go."

Beth seconded the motion. I was to drive them to the movie, and Beth's mother would pick them up afterward.

Bobby spent the next half hour in the bathroom, giving the soap, toothpaste, deodorant, and hair spray a workout like they'd never had before. He came out looking and smelling like a walking advertisement for Ivory Soap.

"Why don't you put on some aftershave?" teased Steven, thoroughly enjoying the situation.

Ignoring his brother, Bobby ran out to the car. By the time I joined him there a few minutes later, every scrap of paper had been removed from the floor and the seats. The car had *never* looked so good.

After we picked up Beth, she and Bobby stared at each other self-consciously for a few minutes. Then suddenly they relaxed and began chatting away as if I had vanished.

They compared notes about how much money they had brought along (this was a "dutch date"), what kind of candy they planned to buy, and how eager they were to see the movie—which they each had seen twice before.

I dropped them off at the corner of the movie theater and watched them walk along the street together: Bobby looking tall and manly, Beth looking petite and feminine; both of them looking pleased with themselves, each other, and the world.

Now, Bobby is Bob—actually "Dr. Bob"—and he has three children. I'm not even sure that Bob and Beth remember each other's names. But I have a feeling that they will always remember the special Sunday afternoon when they went on a "kind of, sort of, almost *first* date."

Arlene Uslander

"I think Ben loves me.
He asked me to share his cubby with him."

True Love!

My parent's fifteenth anniversary passed just last week. They hugged and laughed and held each other tight. So many beautiful words kept flowing out of my dad's mouth, "I love you, Hallye. I really love you."

People throw love away every day, but watching my parents' love amazed me. They stayed together through all of the rough times and challenges that came their way. They always look to each other when they are feeling down or just need someone to talk to.

I worried about them divorcing, but they always told me, "*That* will never happen."

I feel so blessed that my parents are so madly in love. When I think of true, down-to-earth love, I think of my parents. I hope that one day, by the grace of God, I will love someone so deeply.

> *Love is patent, love is kind. It does not envy, it does not boast, it is not proud. It is not rude, it is not self-seeking, it is not easily angered, it keeps no record of wrong. Love does not delight in evil, but rejoices with the truth. It*

always protects, always trusts, always hopes, always perseveres." (1 Corinthians 13:4–7 NIV)

My parents truly love each other even in the little things. A few nights ago I caught my parents wrapped around each other slow dancing to their favorite song. They had just finished a big argument, but instead of remaining angry they chose to make up. It takes a lot of *love* for that to happen.

True love is not a high school fling; it is something that cannot be explained. It is *everything!* It becomes your life once you find it.

Katie Knight

Northern Tissue Curves

I have had many crushes: Billy, who was so cute, didn't even cry when he fell out of a tree in the play area outside our kindergarten classroom. Johnny, in third grade, could do backward flips off the high bar and could even beat the older kids in tetherball. But it wasn't till the summer between fifth and sixth grade that I really fell in love.

David had dark, wavy hair, broad shoulders, and an easy smile. Our mothers had been best friends growing up. Every summer, when our family vacationed in Arizona, we visited his family. He took my older sister, Sharon, and me on horseback rides, he on his bay quarter horse, Sharon and I on his father's Shetland ponies.

That summer, Lee, one of David's friends, walked with us to the barn to saddle up. We hadn't met him before, and I watched Sharon and him ogle each other. Sharon was fourteen and had hazel eyes, long auburn hair, and already sported a good figure. Lee was clearly impressed.

I looked at David, and right before my eyes he changed from an old friend to the Marlboro man, tall and lean in his felt cowboy hat and plaid shirt, though, of course, no cigarette. He was fifteen, and I knew that I must be a mere child in his eyes. Still, I could always hope to impress him.

When we returned home, Sharon started writing Lee. I gathered my nerve and started writing David.

David wrote back. My heart flip-flopped every time I saw his left-slanted handwriting on an envelope addressed to me. In a letter that came right after Valentine's Day, he wrote that he and Lee were coming to Los Angeles to spend spring break with Lee's relatives. My parents arranged to pick up the boys one afternoon at Lee's cousin's house and drop the four of us kids at a movie. Sharon and I started counting the days till our double date.

In preparation, Sharon tried on every dress in her closet and all her lipsticks, turning this way and that before her dresser mirror. She finally chose a green sheath and a cherry lipstick. She looked terrific. We decided on a powder blue polished-cotton dress with a scooped neck and a wide navy blue cummerbund for me. She painted my lips a soft pink my parents might not notice. I didn't look too bad, but my plain old blue eyes, mousy hair, and the beginnings of prepubescent acne bothered me. What could I do to capture David's heart?

The day we were to see David and Lee, we spent all morning getting ready. Sharon turned a slow circle in front of me. "How do I look?" she asked.

"Perfect. What about me?"

Sharon narrowed her eyes and studied me. She tightened my cummerbund and poofed the bodice of my dress above it, then stepped back and studied me some more. "Are you wearing your training bra?" she asked.

She and I both knew I didn't need it yet.

"Get the bra," she said.

Obediently I took off my dress and put on the training bra. Once more Sharon cinched and poofed, then disappeared into the bathroom and returned with a roll of toilet paper. As fast as I could tear off bits of tissue, she put them inside my training bra, pushing here, poking there, till I had the semblance of a figure. I felt awkward and embarrassed, but Sharon assured me that David would like what he saw.

I wore a white cardigan when we left the house to conceal from my parents my David-designed look. The drive to pick up the boys went smoothly. Mother rode in front with my father, so Lee and David had to crowd in the back seat of our '56 Plymouth with Sharon and me. My heart rate doubled. When we got to the movie, the boys piled out first. David offered his hand to help me out. I felt ecstatically happy as I walked down the street with him, Sharon and Lee in front of us, carefully waiting to hold hands till my parents were out of sight.

Ecstatically happy, that is, until my father leaned out the window and yelled, "Don't forget, Sammie gets in for a child's fare."

I must have turned bright red. *Would David now see a big number "eleven" on my chest when he looked at me, instead of my new, alluring shape?*

When we settled into our seats, Sharon and I next to each other, the boys on either side, I took off my sweater. Not that David would notice anything in the dark, but when the lights went on in the theater I wanted to look right. We bought popcorn and watched the movie. I don't remember what we saw, but I do remember that David smelled wonderful. *Did he already shave and have on aftershave?* Sometimes our hands bumped as we both reached for the popcorn. Sometimes our shoulders touched.

Afterward we walked to Bob's Hamburgers. I carried my sweater over one arm. My father gave Sharon money to treat the four of us to ice cream or sodas. I felt very grown-up as David and I slid into one side of a red vinyl booth and Sharon and Lee slid into the other. I was a young woman on a date.

A waitress handed us all menus. As I ran my eyes down the page, I felt someone kick my shins under the table. I looked up and caught Sharon's eye. She pointed at the front of her dress. "You look fine," I mouthed and resumed reading.

Sharon kicked me again. This time she pointed to the front of my dress.

Lee, beside her, glanced at me, then quickly away, then back, as if he couldn't quite keep his eyes off me but was really trying.

Had I spilled something on my dress? I hadn't even ordered yet. Did I have a smear of butter from the popcorn? I tucked my chin and looked down, but I couldn't see anything very clearly above the wide cummerbund.

Sharon motioned toward the restroom and stood up. I stood up, too, leaving my sweater on the seat, and David moved so I could get out. I followed Sharon into the bathroom where she said, simply, "Look." I walked over to the mirror above the sink. Three pieces of toilet paper had worked their way out of my training bra and wriggled into view above the scooped neckline of my dress.

I covered my mouth with my hands and stared in horror. *What could I do?*

I would far rather die than face David again. There was no window in the bathroom for a quick escape. If I did find a way to sneak past him and make it to the sidewalk, I was much too far from home to walk. Besides, David's family and ours would gather for their annual celebration in a few months. I'd have to face him then.

So I needed to return to the table and pretend nothing happened. I could either remove every shred of toilet paper and exit the bathroom flat-chested, or push everything back into place and hope for better luck during the next hour.

Repadding my training bra was just too risky. I prodded

and picked till every bit of tissue was gone. Then Sharon and I puffed my dress up around the cummerbund. If miracles actually happened, David wouldn't notice that anything of interest above my waist had completely disappeared.

David and Lee must have done all their laughing while we were in the bathroom. When we returned, they asked us some questions about the movie, as though they'd been discussing it all the time we were gone. The four of us ordered chocolate malts and somehow I drank mine. Somehow I climbed back in the car when my parents picked us up and told them we'd had a fabulous time.

And somehow, when Sharon got a letter from David telling her he'd had a mad crush on her for years, I didn't cry. Some day, when I filled out a bra with me, not Northern Tissue, I would find love again.

Samantha Waltz

Daddy's Home!

A truly rich man is one whose children run into his arms when his hands are empty.

Source Unknown

I remember vividly when my daddy went off to World War II. Oh, how I missed him. The tune "Sentimental Journey," to this day, plunges me into syrupy-sweet melancholy that, *click,* transports me onto the floor of our mill village house in front of a four-foot-high cabinet radio, my ear pressed to its grill-covered speaker. I am four. Mama is lying across the bed, weeping softly because she misses Daddy, too.

I don't know where Germany is, except that it's far away and Daddy's there. I forget sometimes that Daddy is gone. When the mill whistle blows at shift changes, I run to the front doorsteps, sit, peering eagerly for Daddy to crest the hill, and grin when he sees me. I don't like to forget—it makes Mama cry more.

Sometimes, we go to PaPa and Two-Mama's house for a few days. Going there makes me squeal and leap with rapture.

Click. I catapult to nighttime at my grandparents' house. Baby brother Jimmy and I lie in the bed we share with Mama. From an open fireplace, crackling flames warm and wash the dim, cozy chamber golden. Mama, seated in the big oak rocking chair, writes on a tablet in her lap—her nightly letter to Daddy—pausing only to refill her pen's tip from an ink bottle perched on the chair arm. A soft knock on the cottage's front door does not deter her reverent communiqué. Nor does her father's quiet words to the late visitor.

Not until he calls to her, "Irene—it's James."

Daddy? I jackknife upright in bed as Mama springs up, bare feet already moving her swiftly from the room. Startled, I gaze at tablet, pen, and ink bottle crashing to the floor in the wake of her hummingbird-like departure. I quickly scoot from the covers and pad barefoot to the doorway and spy the exuberant reunion.

Stunning in his army uniform, my handsome Daddy sweeps Mama into his arms and lifts her from the floor, swinging her round and round as they kiss. Excitement hums out my fingers and toes as he finally lowers her to her feet and turns to look at me. He stares at me for a long time, his mouth slowly curling up at the corners as his blue-gray eyes form glimmering half-moons of joy. Then suddenly, I'm in his arms and he's nuzzling my neck and covering my cheeks with kisses.

Daddy's home! I'm so happy I want to shriek and twirl and leap up and touch a big piece of sky. But I'm too overcome with awe and shyness, and instead wrap my small arms around his neck and squeeze as tightly as I can, inhaling his spicy scent, one that will forever represent manhood to me.

Later, he takes me on his lap. There, with his minty breath ruffling my cotton-top hair, he tells a story: "Overseas, I thought about my little Susie every day." His dulcet baritone scatters goose bumps over me.

"You used to play on the screened-in back porch, entertaining yourself with the simplest things. And always with this wide grin on your face. You especially liked piling up little pebbles and rocks and then dropping them one by one into an empty milk bottle."

He sighs. "We—Mama and I—were potty training you along about that time. You were doing pretty good, and I was so proud of you. Then one day I walked out on the back porch where you'd been playing earlier." His arms tighten around me and I snuggle closer.

"That's when I saw it—it seemed you'd had an accident. Right there on the floor." His fingers move slowly to my small hand. He closes it inside his and squeezes it gently. "Aggravated, I rushed back inside and called to you." He stops, and I hear him swallow. "'I here, Daddy,' you called back. I found you playing in your room, this time with buttons and bottle tops, doing your little thing with them in a basket. I spanked you for your accident. And tears washed away your smile."

"Then I went to the back porch to clean up your accident. I discovered I had mistaken the 'accident' for your little pile of pebbles." His voice is now deep and guttural. "I felt like crawling into a hole and never coming out." He holds me so firmly, I cannot see his face. Anyway, I don't want to move from this coziness, so I just ride the momentum of his heaving chest.

Long moments go by before he speaks hoarsely again. "I was in France when the memory of it really hit me. It was Christmas Day and bitterly cold. Snow covered everything. I missed my family. Most of all, I thought of Susie. And her smile. And how I'd spanked her so unjustly. I cried and moped until one of my buddies sent the company chaplain in to me."

"What did he say?" Mama asks, gently fingering his coat's brass buttons.

"He told me to forgive myself. That my little girl had already forgotten it and wouldn't want her Daddy to feel bad."

Now he loosens his hold until I can look up and see him. He gazes at me through tears.

"Don't cry, Daddy," I say through wobbly lips.

"I'm so sorry, Susie." His words come out choked. His face looks like it hurts.

I wipe tears from my cheeks. "What for, Daddy?"

Something flickers in his eyes. Then they light up. "For being such a dope."

A grin slowly breaks over Daddy's face, and he hugs me to him again, along with Mama, and the three of us inhale each other for long moments before bursting into giggles and belly laughs.

Today, I sigh with contentment as the picture fades, because I still feel the honey-warm comfort his strong arms provided and the serenity gleaned from hearing his deep, rich voice rumbling anything intelligible. I still experience velvety, cocoon-wrapped security just knowing, beyond a morsel of doubt, that Mama and Daddy loved each other.

Yet the sweetest comfort of all is knowing Daddy cared.

Emily Sue Harvey

First Comes Love

One particularly warm spring morning, my kids went out to play and came home with little fistfuls of tiny white wriggly creatures. As the oldest unclenched his fist, he asked, "What are they, Mom?"

I tried not to look disgusted as I explained to him, and to his sibs, that they each held in their hands, gobs of baby flies, otherwise known as maggots.

My kids were not instantly mortified at this news, so I gave "the talk" about flies, filth, colds, flu, and germs in general.

Somehow subjects of our dog's personal eating and grooming habits, getting licked by the dog, and kissing others came up. Not stomaching this any longer, I rattled off a few facts about how filthy the human mouth is and desperately hoped that this disgusting information would not only quiet my children, but also send them headlong into the bathroom to wash their hands and, while they were at it, brush their teeth. They just giggled and scurried back outside. Suddenly, it occurred to me they had not washed their hands. I desperately called after them to come back and wash their hands . . . too late; I don't think they heard me.

A few minutes later, I looked out the window and saw my kids rounding the corner. Apparently, they were taking the neighbors stroller for a spin. *How sweet,* I mused, so I grabbed some crackers for the baby I assumed they were strolling and headed after the kids. Then I remembered how they hadn't washed their hands and shuddered at the thought of them now spreading germs all over the neighbor's adorable little angel. So I also grabbed a fistful of disinfectant wipes on my way out the door.

As I got closer, I could hear them chanting that timeless childhood tune, "First comes love, then comes marriage . . ."

My oldest daughter cut in as she stuck out her tongue, "*Oh, gross!* That means they kissed."

I giggled to myself, thinking how the kids groaned and rolled up their eyes each time their dad and I kissed each other.

When I'd caught up to the kids, I asked about the baby and started handing out antibacterial towelettes.

Somebody giggled.

Suspicious, I pulled back the blanket. I beheld a great big glob of maggots on the seat.

"We're taking the babies for a walk," they announced in unison.

"*Oh, gross!*" I moaned.

When my husband arrived home that night, I gave him an especially great big gloppy, sloppy kiss—right in front of my kids.

"*Oh, gross!*" they announced in unison.

To this day, my family reminisces fondly, "First comes love, then comes marriage, then comes maggots in a baby carriage."

When someone will kiss a spouse or potential spouse, everyone will giggle and roar, "*Oh, gross!*" in unison.

Jacqueline Michels

The Kiss

He is not a lover who does not love forever.

Euripides

I was playing Candy Land at my friend's house one Saturday afternoon. We had just finished our third game and went into the kitchen to stretch and to eat some chocolate ice cream. My friend's parents didn't hear us come in. Her father went up to her mother and kissed her smack on the lips.

I gasped. I wondered if we should run back into my friend's room so they wouldn't see us.

But my friend just went to the refrigerator and got the container of ice cream out of the freezer as if nothing had happened. Her mother looked at us and smiled.

"Whoops," she said.

Her father laughed and walked out of the room.

"Do you need help?" her mother asked.

"No, thanks," said my friend. "We're just going to make sundaes."

"Okay," her mother said, and then she left, too.

"Did you see that?" I whispered.

"What?" my friend asked.

"Your parents were kissing!"

"Oh, they do that all the time. Do you want chocolate syrup or whipped cream or both?"

I took both and some chopped walnuts on top, too. I'm sure it tasted good, but I wasn't paying much attention to my sundae right then. I was thinking about the kiss. My parents never did that—at least not in front of my sister or me. I wondered if they kissed at all. Wasn't that what grownups did when they loved each other?

So I started watching my parents. I didn't want to miss the kiss in case they did it. One day I saw my father pat my mother on her shoulder. Mom smiled at him. She seemed to like it. But it wasn't a kiss.

Now I began to worry. Maybe my parents didn't love each other anymore and that's why they didn't kiss.

Another day I noticed that Mom gave my father a hug on her way to do the wash. I think I heard him say, "Mmmm," but I wasn't certain. They both looked happy, yet it still wasn't a kiss.

"Do you and Daddy still love each other?" I asked Mom as I helped her fold the clean laundry.

"Of course," she said.

"Are you sure?"

"I'm sure."

Maybe this love thing was more complicated than I realized.

One Sunday morning, when the sun was just beginning to peek through the windows, I woke up hungry and quietly went into the kitchen to get a bowl of cereal. And then I saw them. Mom and Dad were just coming out of their bedroom. They stopped in the doorway and kissed! It wasn't the kiss on the cheek kind of kiss that they gave me. It wasn't the quick kiss in the kitchen kind of kiss that

I saw at my friend's house. It was a mouth-to-mouth slurpy kiss that lasted a long time.

Ewww, I thought.

I sneaked back to my room. I guessed my parents really did love each other if they could kiss like that.

But I never wanted to see it again.

Ferida Wolff

"If you ask me, he's gonna get germs. I know it's already given me the willies."

A Gift from Heaven

My grandpa died a few years ago, and it broke my grandma's heart. Just recently on Valentine's Day, she sat in her backyard with her dog, thinking about how much she missed Grandpa.

She lives on the top of a hill, and while she was looking down on the buildings below her house, suddenly out of nowhere a balloon flew right into her hands. It was shaped like a heart and on it were spelled the words "I love you."

Alison Kay Kennedy

6

INSIGHTS AND LESSONS

Life is just a chance to grow a soul.

A. Powell Davies

The Beauty of a Dull Glow

Immature love says: I love you because I need you. Mature love says: I need you because I love you.

Erich Fromm

My hands reluctantly approach the task, dip into soapy water, then give in to the repetition. Soon purple and green water bottles drip upside down, knives dry, and bowls rise up to form an imposing mound in the dish drainer. Briefly interrupting my sudsy meditation, I let out the dirty water and swish the sink clean. Again, I fill the sink with bubbles. The final act begins and ends with pots and pans. I scrub, glancing at them. I notice that the six-quart pan seems dull beside the shiny new four-quart pan.

The bigger pan, used these ten years of marriage, reflects my image dully, without definite shape. My face peers back, mirrorlike, from the smaller pan. I suddenly remember the comments long-married women made at my bridal showers: "I wish I could get married again so I could get all new towels and pots." "Must be nice to start with all new things." As if the men to whom they remained married weren't a gift enough.

Of course, now that I've been married for what qualifies these days as a long time, I like to receive new things once in a while. But many items I possess work just fine, even if they are a bit old—especially my husband, and I hope he thinks the same of me.

Recently I read an article about a therapist who thinks that the institution of marriage has become utterly obsolete. He isn't the first to make this bold pronouncement, and he certainly won't be the last. Not only can women support themselves financially, say these marital naysayers, but modern mobility issues complicate a couple's ability to stay together. Reading between the lines, I got the message that if something owned is not fresh anymore, just shop for a replacement; it's cheaper to replace than to repair or maintain.

But my old pots and pans still work well. We only added a different size to our already functional set. It's amazing what these pots represent in our years of marriage: learning to merge his and mine into ours, and the old with the new; the tradition of Christmas Eve soups and candlelight dinners using china pieces we received as gifts; the switch to simple meals in the months after becoming new parents; the gatherings with our extended family; and the day-to-day life of a love that changed, matured, and continues to hold steady.

Crow's feet appear. Bellies grow Rubenesque. First one, then several gray hairs pepper my husband's black curly hair. I am no longer that glowing bride, nor he the grinning groom. We are tired of fixing meals, rounding up children, paying bills, washing dishes, and having so little left for each other at the end of the day. Oh, but our lives are so full. I watch my husband substitute words in storybooks only to be caught by emerging readers. He sees me handle the details of our daily lives and remembers when I barely could cover the fine points of my own schedule.

I mourn the times we spent alone, yet revel in this season filled with children and activities and exhaustion. Who else has watched me give birth? Who did not shy away from the sometimes overwhelming responsibilities associated with raising twins? And did I not stand by while his family's business difficulties invaded our own home?

We could have walked away from it all—to find a little romance in flirting with newness that did not involve our shared histories. Just as everyday life brings wear and tear to pots and pans, it can be equally hard on long-term relationships. We long for a world away from it all, and yet, that world is an illusion. Every new relationship that has any value will eventually become an old relationship.

We can keep cleaning and polishing our pans or we can give them to charity. That shiny new pan looks attractive and enhances the set we already own. However, it doesn't make me want to give away what I already have. Just like our other pans, it will scratch up and lose its luster. But, still, it will cook our food just fine.

My old pans aren't obsolete and neither is my marriage.

Trina Lambert

Love Is Easy; Married Is Hard

Love is easy . . . married is hard. In the days before thoughts of a wedding filled my mind, male suitors wearing floppy-brimmed Woodstock hats arrived at my door, offering lavish boxes of chocolates and romantic record albums like Mel Torme's *Torch Songs*. Some artfully presented a long-stemmed rose accompanied by a poem, something erotic by Leonard Cohen or Irving Layton. One admirer insisted on penning his own poetry—he should have let the experts wax poetic on his behalf.

Before nuptials the days were filled with moonlit drives in the country, endless conversations murmured over countless cups of coffee, romantic dinners left uneaten because our hands had more important things to do. (How did we drive a standard clutch, grip a dripping ice cream cone, and hold hands all at the same time?) Inconveniences like sleeping and eating were barely tolerated because they interrupted time spent together.

Love, a frenzied, frantic business, so excited me that it made my stomach sick. The fire raged, the heart exploded, and putting two rational thoughts together was a Herculean effort.

And then I married. Not once, but twice. My first marriage gave me lots of opportunity to learn new skills—like how to whip up Three Cheese Hamburger Helper, make my toilet fixtures glisten, and sanitize my floor so that we could eat off it when the holidays rolled around.

After I married for the second time, gifts on Valentine's Days and wedding anniversaries officially marked our love. Spontaneous offerings of floppy, Bob Dylan–like hats, long stemmed roses, and Mel Torme albums collected dust in the linen closet. On our first anniversary, my husband bought me a frilly nightgown that couldn't keep a bug warm. On our second anniversary, my husband bought me a pair of flannel pajamas with a turtleneck. On our third anniversary, he gave me a Dust Buster. It was downhill after that.

It's now year thirty-seven of my second marriage. I just turned sixty-two. My first marriage lasted about five years, ended badly, and made a flock of lawyers a lot of money. I am thankful that there are no offspring from that "flower child" marriage of the '60s. Ex-husband and I are not good friends, as popular and civilized as the practice may be. However, I no longer have the uncontrollable urge to run him over with my Volvo. I consider this a huge step.

Husband number two is a whole different story. Thirty-seven years together speaks volumes. Our passion still burns, but it glows rather than singes; the endless conversation is punctuated with intervals of comfortable silence; we still hold hands in the movies; he picks up flowers at Safeway, but the point is, he still buys them. As for me, I prefer to shop for my own hats and nighties.

Appliances remain officially crossed off our mutual gift lists, and jewelry has replaced chocolates. (My cholesterol level is way too high!) Any piece of new software, or a CD by Lyle Lovett pleases "the mister." Sounds dull, I suppose, but it's not. It's love with less flash and less sizzle, I guess—and it's less mercurial than the old days. Its constancy, its solidity, its safety, and its equal component of friends and lovers combine our thirty-seven-year-long love into an amalgam from which soul mates are forged.

Sometimes I think we should wear matching bowling jackets, except we don't bowl. We finish each other's sentences or give voice to a thought the other hasn't spoken. It's spooky. My thirty-four-year-old daughter, the gift of this marriage, observed that her father and I are starting to look alike. Now, that's really spooky!

But the truth is, that's what soul mates are like. In the Broadway musical *Fiddler on the Roof*, Tevye asks Golde, after forty-five years of marriage, "Do you love me?" Golde is flummoxed—it's something she truly never thought about. At song's end, when both declare, "It doesn't change a thing," the strength of their love no longer remains a question in their minds, or in ours. We have no doubt about their love for each other and how deeply it sustains them.

Blessedly, like Golde, neither do I.

Sharon Melnicer

When the Right One Comes Along

I always felt that the great high privilege, relief, and comfort of friendship was that one had to explain nothing.

Katherine Mansfield

Once in a lifetime, if we're lucky, someone comes along—someone who makes us aware that maybe, just maybe, things happen for reasons we don't understand. Things outside of our control that breathe magic into our lives in ways we never thought possible.

For me, that someone is Mitchel.

I'd like to say that when we first met sparks flew, but that isn't the way the story unfolded. At that time, I was very lonely. My three children, whom I reared alone, were out in the world doing wonderful, productive things. My home was an empty nest. And to make matters worse, the sweetness of the relationship I thought would be my "happily ever after" turned sour: I lived alone, nursing a broken heart.

One bright spot in my life was my job as the training

and development manager at the Humane Society Silicon Valley. An oddity among the staff, I was the only employee without an animal companion. Although I was still a little wary of relationships, I made the decision to adopt a shelter dog: mature, quiet, intellectual. Sort of a canine Gregory Peck.

As is often the case, things didn't go according to plan. A year after I made the decision, I was still dogless; none caught my eye or, more important, touched my heart.

Until that cold, wet September day.

I made my daily rounds through the kennels, something I did three or four times a day. Now that might sound excessive, obsessive even, but conditions can change quickly at the shelter. Ralph the pit bull in Kennel 109 at 10 AM might be replaced by Sugar the poodle at 2 PM Dogs moved in and out that quickly, and I wanted to be in the right place at the right time. I wanted first dibs.

Although I wasn't quite sure whether my dream dog would be a Ralph or a Sugar, I knew one thing: when the right one came along, I would recognize him or her.

Shaved, shaking, and pitifully sad when I first spotted him in the kennel, he looked more like a soulful hound than a tenacious terrier. Plastered against the far left-hand corner of the kennel, he refused to acknowledge my presence. This dejected little guy looked as though he had lost his best friend, and after seeing the sorrowful eyes of so many abandoned animals during my days at the shelter, I knew that was most likely the case. I tried frantically to get his attention to let him know that he was going to be okay, that he was now in the care of people who cared, really cared. I whistled, hoping the sound would catch his ear. I waved, hoping the movement would catch his eye. As a last resort, I poked a slice of hot dog through the fence.

No luck. This mournful mutt wasn't going to throw me a bone.

I dashed upstairs to my cubicle and logged on to the Chameleon database:

Mitchel. #A396462
TRICOLOR & GRAY
FOX TERR WIRE
4 yrs 0.26 mos.
Neutered

The records showed he'd had two previous owners; both had abandoned him.

By the time I finished reading his profile and typed "Put on Hold," I was smitten with this little wirehair fox terrier named Mitchel. I've always fallen for a guy with a mustache and big brown eyes. I raced back down to the kennels and assured the man of my dreams that all was well. Within the next seventy-two hours, I accompanied him through his behavior and health testing. I learned that he had a "soft mouth," a rather skittish temperament, and a strong dislike for cats.

Upon receiving word of Mitchel's adoption stamp of approval, I beckoned counselor Christina Cabrera to perform the honors. With adoption papers signed, sealed, and delivered, I marched my new main squeeze into AlphaPet and bought the store: dog chow, food dish, matching water dish, plaid collar, matching leash, furry squeaky toy, and a midsize Greenie.

After all, my man deserved the best.

I spent the next two weekends checking out local veterinarians, boarding kennels, groomers, and dog parks. Decisions made, we settled in. All went well until the following week. On our daily walk, I noticed Mitchel was urinating blood.

I rushed him to his vet, fearful of the news I might receive. After a battery of tests, nothing showed up. Dr.

Douglas recommended an X-ray. Puzzle solved. My twenty-two-pound terrier carried three bladder stones each the size of Mars. Or so it seemed after viewing the X-ray.

Mitchel underwent surgery the next morning.

Three days later, I picked him up from the hospital. His wounds and stitches were extensive, but he remained rather stoic. He continued to heal without incident for another week. And then it happened again. This time blood was coming from his right ear. After extensive poking and prodding, Dr. Douglas discovered a deep ear infection that Mitchel had for quite some time. He went into surgery, and again, I took him home to heal.

It was during the second round of cleansing, applying salve, and administering medications that I began to take notice of Mitchel's personality: He displayed characteristics of courage and bravery—something that told the world that nothing, absolutely nothing, kept him from healing his broken body or his broken heart.

The saying, "When the pupil is ready, the teacher will appear," spoke volumes about my life with Mitchel. It was no accident that he came into my life at that very moment. A time when I needed to learn about healing.

And as the days passed, it became more and more obvious that this furry little fellow was going to be my teacher.

Mitchel and I have been together for almost three years now. Bladders and ears are now healed. We're both healthy, happy, and continuing to learn how to live together successfully. I like to think that I gave Mitchel a new "leash" on life by providing him with excellent health care, hearty food, an unlimited supply of love, and shelter from the storm.

I can say with absolute certainty that he, in turn, gave me a new perspective on living. He taught me that each and every morning there is a wonderful world outside just waiting to be explored. Even if I travel the same path day after day, there is always something new to sniff out. All I need to do is get out of bed, put on my clothes, and head out.

He taught me the delights of mealtime—that good food heals the body as well as the heart. Even if it's the same menu day after day, I can enjoy and savor food—glorious food—especially peanut butter on a spoon.

He taught me that rolling in freshly cut grass can awaken my senses in a way that I never thought possible.

He taught me that chasing after something, even if I never catch it, is an exhilarating experience. He has yet to catch a cat or a squirrel, but ah, the chase.

He taught me that napping is an art—especially on a Sunday afternoon when I should be doing something far more important.

He taught me that sleeping on the same bed with someone you love keeps the nightmares at bay.

He taught me that it's okay to have my sights set on a Gregory Peck, but to go with the flow if a Will Ferrell comes into my life instead.

And, most of all, he taught me that my heart, although broken, continues to mend each and every time I tousle that mustache and look into those big brown eyes.

Patricia Smith

"Sounds like puppy love."

Fireworks

She presses her head against my shoulder. "Beautiful, isn't it?" she whispers. It's not a question. I wrap my arms around her tightly, resting my head on top of hers. "Yeah, I guess it kinda is."

But I don't see what is so amazing about it.

She had dragged me all the way to Apsley to go onto the roof of her cottage, which is where we now sit. I shiver, and glance at my watch—it's after midnight.

How long do we have to sit up here and stare at nothing?

I pull her tighter to me in a failing attempt to keep warm. Her dark blue eyes are permanently glued to the sky, and again I look up to try to see what she is so awed by. Tiny lights flicker above us, and every five seconds they are momentarily shielded by a flash of neon colors when the people across the lake set off their fireworks.

It's like we've never seen fireworks before.

Glancing back down at her, I notice for the first time how each color reflects itself on her pale white skin. I watch as her face glows a brilliant hue of green and then red and finally blue, which always suited her best. Her

READER/CUSTOMER CARE SURVEY

We care about your opinions! Please take a moment to fill out our online Reader Survey at **http://survey.hcibooks.com.**
As a **"THANK YOU"** you will receive a **VALUABLE INSTANT COUPON** towards future book purchases as well as a **SPECIAL GIFT** available only online! Or, you may mail this card back to us and we will send you a copy of our exciting catalog with your valuable coupon inside.

(PLEASE PRINT IN ALL CAPS)

First Name _____ MI. _____ Last Name _____

Address _____ City _____

State _____ Zip _____ Email _____

1. Gender
☐ Female ☐ Male

2. Age
☐ 8 or younger ☐ 13-16
☐ 9-12 ☐ 17-20 ☐ 21-30
☐ 31+

3. Did you receive this book as a gift?
☐ Yes ☐ No

4. Annual Household Income
☐ under $25,000
☐ $25,000 - $34,999
☐ $35,000 - $49,999
☐ $50,000 - $74,999
☐ over $75,000

5. What are the ages of the children living in your house?
☐ 0 - 14 ☐ 15+

6. Marital Status
☐ Single
☐ Married
☐ Divorced
☐ Widowed

7. How did you find out about the book?
(please choose one)
☐ Recommendation
☐ Store Display
☐ Online
☐ Catalog/Mailing
☐ Interview/Review

8. Where do you usually buy books?
(please choose one)
☐ Bookstore
☐ Online
☐ Book Club/Mail Order
☐ Sports
☐ Price Club (Sam's Club, Costco's, etc.)
☐ Retail Store (Target, Wal-Mart, etc.)

9. What subject do you enjoy reading about the most?
(please choose one)
☐ Parenting/Family
☐ Relationships
☐ Recovery/Addictions
☐ Health/Nutrition

☐ Christianity
☐ Spirituality/Inspiration
☐ Business Self-help
☐ Women's Issues
☐ Sports

10. What attracts you most to a book?
(please choose one)
☐ Title
☐ Cover Design
☐ Author
☐ Content

TAPE IN MIDDLE; DO NOT STAPLE

BUSINESS REPLY MAIL

FIRST-CLASS MAIL PERMIT NO 45 DEERFIELD BEACH, FL

POSTAGE WILL BE PAID BY ADDRESSEE

Chicken Soup for the Soul®
3201 SW 15th Street
Deerfield Beach FL 33442-9875

FOLD HERE

Comments

Do you have your own Chicken Soup story
that you would like to send us?
Please submit at: **www.chickensoup.com**

eyes shimmer in a vortex of hues, but it's the moments in between the flashes, the moments when everything fades to black and only the glow of the moon illuminates her, the moments when she unconsciously presses herself tighter to me, jumping at the smallest howl in the distance, that make me catch my breath.

"Are you cold?" she asks, noticing how my whole body is shaking. "We can go in now, it doesn't really matter to me." I shake my head, kiss her, and whisper, "Maybe we can stay out—a bit longer?"

Allie M. Hill

My Love Story

The aim of life is to live, and to live means to be aware, joyously, drunkenly, serenely, divinely aware.

Henry Miller

Our chance encounter set in motion events that combined the delicate balance between instinct, knowledge, and desire.

Instantly and mutually we were surprised and challenged by a force we only heard of: love at first sight.

Emotions and events unfolded rapidly and filled with intense purpose.

Together we agreed to follow a course of action totally determined by this mysterious power.

Both of us were willing to travel the course, accept the challenge, and risk the outcome.

We chose to create a relationship, with the hope that it would last a lifetime.

We knew the criteria for success: honesty, communication, belief and trust in each other, and a desire for passion that would endure a lifetime.

We agreed to explore this new frontier, to discover the whirlwind of emotions, giddy joys, and pleasures along the way, to give unfaltering attention to each other.

We proceeded without fear or worry.

We believed in what we were about to embark upon— this true, time-tested ritual.

Our courtship, like so many others, was colorful, exciting, and rewarding.

Many moments of tenderness and understanding provoked amazing and unexpected responses to the poetic and melodic insights of love.

Often we experienced wishful and magical moments through childlike views of beauty and truth.

We shared and appreciated exchanges of special glances, gentle touches, stolen kisses, and secret confessions.

We shared aspirations of grandeur and the overall natural splendor of the path we chose.

All these things grew and developed into the "I do" as our partnership began.

We took time to savor special moments, to give birth to an external passion that would later establish a family legacy: five children.

Time passed without warning as attention to marital details manifested themselves.

Although plans were not always easily carried out and often interrupted by life's unpredictable events, we forged ahead.

We worked thirty-eight years at making our relationship sustain its original vows.

During the process doubts and questions arose, continuity and endurance faltered, fear of rejection, loneliness, separation, and seclusion appeared, and we struggled.

Yet, throughout all difficulties, we persevered.

We reflected back over time and clung to the original attraction of the past: love at first sight.

Again we shared the same individual and personal admiration for each other; we renewed the promises and concerns that began the process so we could continue.

Our love resisted life's interruptions and held steadfast.

The love that at one time appeared as strange, mystical, and magical, which acquired a life of its own and took us both to the limits and beyond, endured a lifetime.

True, its path encountered hardships, but was overpowered with joy and happiness.

So as the English poet Alexander Pope wrote: "A little learning is a dangerous thing; drink deep, or taste not the Pierian spring."

When that special someone comes your way, enjoy every moment fully, hold dear the memories, for they will sustain and help you remember romance and never forget love.

Helen Colella

A Babe in Boyland

Your task is not to seek for love, but merely to seek and find all the barriers within yourself that you have built against it.

Rumi

I squealed with joy as happy tears splashed on my go-go boots. The Beatles were on the Ed Sullivan show, and I watched with enraptured bliss. I knew I was in love with Paul McCartney. I knew that somehow, someway, he would find me and marry me.

An optimist, I was in fourth grade at the time. While I waited for Paul to search for me in Winona, Minnesota, I found a stand-in. Jack, the cutest boy in our class, came to school with a Beatle haircut. Captivated, I never spoke to Jack because he was one of the cool kids. I was only average, in every way except one: I was an excellent schemer.

One morning Jack got in trouble for passing a note to Wendy (another cool kid—she owned a horse) and the teacher sentenced him to after-school detention. That meant he needed to clean all the chalkboard erasers in the entire school. *Ah ha,* I thought, *here's my chance.* I turned relentlessly obnoxious for the rest of the day until I earned my detention.

Jack and I went from room to room, asking the teachers for their blackboard erasers. Then we took them into the janitor's closet, where we fed them into a cleaning machine. With each grinding, swishing sound, with each breath of chalk dust, I fell deeper in love. When his hand brushed against mine, I thought I was going to faint. He started to talk to me as if I was cool, and suddenly I was. The next day, he gave me a note containing the deepest, most meaningful words I had ever read, "I like you." Our romance lasted for several months, until I outgrew him and developed a killer crush on a sixth-grader who looked like Davy Jones of the Monkees.

The summer between sixth and seventh grade, I gave my first kiss to my neighbor, Billy. Well . . . actually, he bought it from me.

I was working outside, pulling weeds in my front yard when Billy careened around the corner on his red Sting-Ray bike. He skidded to a stop in front of me, and said, "I got you somethin'." He held up a little stuffed animal—a mouse.

Billy said, "I heard you tell my sister that you wanted this . . . that you'd do just about anything to get it, so I bought it from her. I'll give it to ya—for a kiss."

Without a hint of hesitation, I leaned over the bike, kissed him full on the lips, grabbed the mouse, and ran. We both got what we wanted—fair trade. My scheming paid off.

My next little caper didn't go as well. By the time I got to high school, I fell crazy in love with Jimmy. I wrote him poem after poem. He said that I was a great writer and, of course, I believed him. But secretly, I wondered if I could keep writing such epic poetry. I was running out of words that rhymed with kiss. One day as I was sitting on my bed, trying to think of a non-offensive rhyme for heart, I heard a breathtaking song on an old Peter, Paul, and Mary album. The lyrics were haunting. My devious mind kicked in to high gear and developed a plan. *He'll never know that I didn't write it. He never listens to folk singers; he's a rock 'n' roll guy—I can get away with it.* I wrote down the first verse to the song and signed my name to it.

Jimmy was amazed at my new creation. He said, "I think you could sell this; it's really, really good!"

"You were my inspiration. It just says how I feel about you—about us," I explained.

A week later, I was riding in the car with my mother when a DJ announced the title of a new hit single. I froze. That was the name of *"my"* poem! The deep, rich voice of Roberta Flack sang about seeing her lover's face and the sun rising in his eyes. Jimmy never spoke to me again.

My scheming began to backfire.

However, I didn't fully learn my lesson until several years later, after I had married Ron, my college sweetheart. Even though I tried to honor my vows, I was still selfish and manipulative; I was a terrible wife. It was only after I almost lost my marriage that I realized the road to love is not a one-way street.

I learned to find joy in helping others and looked for ways to encourage my husband. As he accomplished his goals, he, in turn, helped me accomplish mine. We are now walking down lover's lane as a team, holding hands, side-by-side.

Next year we will celebrate our twenty-ninth anniversary, and the only thing I'm scheming about is how to surprise him with a trip to Hawaii.

Nancy C. Anderson

Love at Sixty Is Different

Meeting you was fate, becoming your friend was a choice, but falling in love with you I had no control.

Source Unknown

"Carol, what you need is a boyfriend," my cousin said as he hauled a computer desk on his back up two flights of stairs to my new apartment.

"Say I wanted a boyfriend," I answered, "which I don't, wanting a boyfriend and finding one at age fifty-eight are two entirely different things."

"You might be surprised," Al said.

I'd been single for seven years since divorcing my second husband. During those seven years I'd reclaimed title to myself as an independent being, with my own strong opinions, strengths, and talents. The day after signing the dissolution papers, I'd bought myself a ring—a small blue sapphire with tiny diamond chips on either side—and made a vow to be true to myself, never again losing my identity behind a man's ego.

"Trust me, you need a boyfriend," Al panted, sweat dripping off the end of his nose as he maneuvered the desk around a tight corner at the top of the stairs.

To prove Al wrong, I placed an ad in the local weekly. I didn't put a lot of effort into the ad: no fancy metaphors, no mention of midnight strolls or watching sunsets at the ocean. I figured I might as well put the age issue right out front so there wouldn't be any misconceptions. My one requirement was compatible politics.

Over the next few weeks I received five responses. The first one was a nonstarter. The second one was too scary to call back. The third one was a wealthy business owner. When I called him back, we talked for an hour and a half and had three more long telephone conversations before we met. He entered Starbucks, wearing a red silk shirt and straw hat. He was whistling, full of humor and energy. John was his name, and I liked him immediately. The coffee date slid into dinner, and the evening wasn't anywhere near long enough to cover everything we wanted to talk about.

Bill was the fourth caller. I met him at a downtown restaurant for Sunday brunch. As I neared the entrance, I saw Bill walking from the opposite direction: a tall, slender man of sixty in a blue parka, wool beret, and a worried look on his face. Conversation was torture. He kept his eyes on his French toast and answered my questions. Yes, he's retired, had been a librarian at the university for twenty-seven years. Silence. He plays classical and jazz guitar. Silence. His politics are liberal, and he's passionately opposed to the current administration. Silence. He graduated from Harvard. Long silence. Finally the plates are cleared and I pick up the check. "No, let me. I invited you," I insist. And then, unexpectedly, I add, "Would you like to get together again?" His face was transformed by a wide, happy grin and sparkling deep blue eyes.

After each of the first eleven dates, I made a decision to see Bill again. I told Al, "There's something there I need to pursue, even though getting to know him is hard work." I've never handled small talk well or been good at thinking up new topics of conversation; but in this relationship I was clearly in the lead—in more ways than one. On the third date, I held his hand. On the seventh, I kissed him.

That was two years ago, and I've learned that love at sixty is different from love at sixteen or thirty-six. By the time we've lived that many years, we've become scarred and careful. We're afraid of falling, knowing how easy it is to trip. Both Bill and I had suffered in relationships and experienced wounds we will carry to our graves. Love at sixty isn't about rearing children, fighting over money, in-laws, or competing for best Christmas lights on the block. It's about companionship and safety. But that doesn't mean it lacks passion. Bill taught me that blind love, generous forgiveness, and unalterable faith can transform the person you love into the person you see through your valentine-colored lenses. As my compulsions and dark family secrets began to surface, he just kept repeating, "You're wonderful; you're beautiful; I'm so lucky to have you in my life." And I started to believe him. He changed the way I see myself and showed me a new way to love. The love I feel for Bill is not jealous or worried. It's like the old hand-knit comforter on my sofa: comforting and familiar.

When Bill and I walk down the street, he holds my hand—not swinging it casually between us, but clutching it high against his chest, near his heart. People who pass us smile. At a Greek restaurant recently, the waitress brought us a plate of baklava at the end of our meal. As we started to protest, she interrupted. "It's on me, because you two are so in love."

Carol Duncan Sweet

Finding My Husband Again

What greater thing is there for human souls than to feel that they are joined for life—to be with each other in silent, unspeakable memories.

Source Unknown

My husband, Bob, and I began a wondrous new journey—all because of a dream. Our love is deeper than ever, though it took over four years to reach this point. By sharing our lessons, I hope others won't have to wait as long as we did for our relationship to heal.

On a cold day in winter, I developed a permanently disabling spinal cord disorder—quite literally overnight. Bob became my round-the-clock caregiver. With our wonderful marriage of twenty-five years, we figured we'd cope beautifully. But we didn't. Neither of us was prepared for what lay ahead.

Because of the disorder, I required a difficult operation. After surgery, we were euphoric that I wasn't completely paralyzed. My neurologist called it "the honeymoon phase." We thought it would last. After all, our entire marriage had been a honeymoon. But soon, reality hit—hard.

Bob had to dress me, clean me, and do every household chore. I felt so guilty, but I didn't tell him. Bob felt over-whelmed, but he didn't tell me. Never wanting me to feel bad, he'd say, "It's nothing," when I thanked him.

Our roles became exclusively caregiver and sick person. *Where did husband and wife go?* I wondered. The distance surfaced in my dreams; not once in four years after the onset of my illness was Bob in any of them.

Instead of reaching out to each other or to friends or to therapists, we metaphorically locked ourselves in self-made emotional isolation rooms. We each would often cry, but kept it barely audible—never wanting to break each other's hearts. If only we would cry and mourn together, our souls could start to heal.

My self-esteem took a nosedive. Once an independent, self-assured woman, I became dependent and insecure. I felt burdensome. I constantly apologized for needing help: "I'm sorry I can't put my socks on by myself."

I longed to talk with Bob. But it seemed more loving not to. I desperately wanted to tell him what living in this defective body was like. I needed to share—to be heard and understood. That's what Bob needed, too. But we both remained silent.

Then a miracle happened. He said, "Last night was the first time I dreamed you were disabled." He became tearful.

I touched his face. "It's fine to cry." Timidly I asked, "How did you feel?"

"The way I have all along: protective." He hung his head. "And powerless to fix you."

"Nobody can." I kept my hand on his face—so needing to touch him—so needing his touch. "It would help if you'd tell me how you're feeling."

"It's hard. I don't want to tell you when I'm exhausted

or my back hurts, you'll feel bad."

"I could rub your back." I held his hand like the lifeline it is. "I've never told you about my feeling like a burden."

"I love taking care of you!" he said. "I want 'us' back."

"Oh, so do I."

"I think we're having a breakthrough." We started laughing through our tears. Then he told me his dream.

"We were on a beach and we *had* to get to an island. I don't know why. There was a boat. I panicked." (He knows no more boats for me. I have no balance.) After a deep cleansing breath, he continued. "A path appeared. We walked across on soil. I held my arms around you so you wouldn't fall, and you held me for support."

We put our arms around each other, as in the dream, but now for emotional support. I said, "You made *our* path,"— I could barely get the precious words out—"on solid ground."

I had never felt anything more profound in my life.

And just as our roles had instantly changed that fateful day long ago, we were no longer caregiver and sick person. We were lovers and best friends.

Bob is now back in my dreams. We finally found our way.

Saralee Perel

Watching from a Doorway

It had been a long, busy night on the med-surg unit. I was making the last check on my quietest patient before going off shift. Coming to the doorway, I saw his wife was still at his side. She had been there all evening. Watching them from the doorway, I hesitated, not wanting to inter-rupt. They held hands and talked quietly, he in bed and she in the chair beside him. Their conversation was filled with pauses. The slow easy murmuring of their exchanges displaced the fear of the sickroom.

He was close to passing and they both knew it. He pat-ted her hand gently as he made a point. She nodded and replied, reaching up to brush the hair off his forehead. These familiar gestures of tenderness came easily to them both. Even as the casual observer, I could see how the love they shared created the peacefulness surrounding them.

A single tear drop escaped and ran down her wrinkled cheek—the only indication of her enormous grief.

She smiled at him through the tear and spoke another brief comment, which made him chuckle. His eyes were on her as she talked, and it was clear there was nothing else more important to him than her. It was the quiet strength of their love that transcended the moment.

As I watched them I understood finally what love really means. I didn't even know it had eluded me until I saw the comfort they offered each other in the face of the inevitable.

Love, I realized, isn't gongs clamoring or the giddy vertigo of adolescents. Rather, it is the calm composure that gives courage to another in the face of overwhelming loss and grief. These two people, soon to be separated, comforted each other in an attempt to make their loss easier. I turned quietly and left, thankful to see the generosity and beauty—of love framed in the tragedy of this event.

Robert D. Russell

Romance

Ideas flow easily from my fingers to the computer screen as I type responses to an e-mail questionnaire. At first I feel obligated to complete the survey because my niece has sent it to me, but I find it's actually kind of fun.

Then I get hit with: "Describe the most romantic moment you and your husband have shared in the last year." My brain freezes. I feel my lower lip protrude the way it does when I'm going into a pout. *Has my marriage included any romantic moments in the past year? When was the last time I prepared a candlelight dinner? The last time Ray surprised me with flowers? I bought my own flowers for Valentine's Day this year, bravely using Ray's credit card, so that in a way they'd be from him.*

Surely we've shared a romantic moment at some point. There is the easy intimacy of a long marriage, but I'm talking something more. I wander out of my office, find Ray working in our garden, and put the question to him. "What, in your opinion, is the most romantic moment we've had recently?"

He looks up, weeding tool in hand. "The most what?"

"The most romantic moment we've had in, say, the past year."

"We've had a lot of romantic moments. Hard to choose just one."

I look at him, grubby T-shirt, stained khakis, the weeding tool slightly bent where he's probably run over it with his car. *He thinks we've had a lot of romantic moments?* My memory flashes something I once read in a women's magazine: if partners widely differ in perception of how things are going, their marriage might be in trouble. *Are we in trouble here?*

I squat beside him. "You really think we've had a lot of romantic moments? Can you give me an example?" I try for a neutral tone, carefully screening out qualities of sarcasm and serious doubt from my voice.

"Sure I can. The way we support each other. That's really romantic." He looks up at me, then back at a stubborn dandelion.

I'm tempted to say, "Now there's a guy for you. Women are from Venus and men are from where?" But I don't. He's so sincere. The answer is foreign to my definition of romance, yet could he have something here?

Is it romantic when I encourage him to take time for himself and go for a hike with a friend? Since he can't seem to let himself otherwise—he is so duty bound—I provide him with his own personal cheering squad. Is it romantic when I hold his hand as we sit in the intensive care unit with his chronically ill son? I hope my presence gives him some comfort. Is it romantic when I join him and his brother and sister-in-law in ministering to his mother as she passes, holding her hand, stroking the white hair at her temples, reassuring her of our love for her? It's such a tender, sweet day for us all. Not moments when sparks fly, but moments when I know both our hearts swell with appreciation for each other.

Is it romantic when Ray attends one of my readings? It might be the third time he's heard the same essays from an anthology, but he's always there, sometimes driving two hours to smile reassuringly from the audience. Is it romantic when I gather a group of friends to play our musical instruments that we haven't touched since high school decades before, and he's sitting close by, grinning and applauding like he's attending the best concert ever? Is it romantic when he changes an appointment to have his car serviced so he can go with me to a pre-op consultation with a plastic surgeon? Removing a skin cancer from near my lower lip should be a simple procedure, but I'm frightened the surgery could be permanently disfiguring. Come to think of it, what more dramatic ways could he show his love?

I look at Ray moving on now to another flowerbed. I go over to him, wrap my arms around him, and press against him. Against his neck I whisper how wonderful he is.

He does have something here. Something better than candlelight dinners and flowers. In the moments when we support each other, it is as though we read each other's heart. We completely accept the values of the other person, focus on each other's well-being and success, and think only of the other's happiness, not our own. What *could* be more romantic?

Samantha Waltz

"Don't pick that! I'm not about to destroy a flower
just to see if you love me or not!"

Marriage with a Firm Foundation

Anyone who tells me about their perfect marriage, I wonder who they're trying to fool. Bill and I have been married forty-eight years, and many of those years were held together by God's glue.

I was a mere child of sixteen and Bill nineteen when we lied about our ages and obtained a marriage license. We grew up together, you might say. Along the way we learned much and experienced both lean years and times of plenty. We learned the art of loving through trial and error. At times we talked, and times we kept silent. We each tugged at our own wills at the expense of the other. We said hurtful words, and we asked for forgiveness. We avoided the obvious, and evaded the truth.

We left to come back. Through the years, many times we thought we fell out of love, only to later discover a new-found excitement, romance, and love for the other. Divorce was a possibility a couple of times when we contemplated our feelings and commitment to each other. We rose above our feelings, for love is more than feelings. Love runs deep below the surface of emotions. Love is a gift to give, not a sentiment to take. Love is a job to work at without ceasing. Love is a friendship that rises above passion.

Our love grew into more than a need. Our love is now as essential as the air we breathe.

We created valleys in our marriage, but out of valleys, mountains rose to *restore* confidence in our union.

Betty King

Love Endures, After All These Years

It is a warm August night—a rather ordinary evening, except it is my wedding anniversary. I have been married to the same man for almost a quarter century, making it an extraordinary evening.

Perhaps we should splurge and buy impressive gifts for each other, but we don't need a thing. Dinner out will work just fine.

Taking a final look in the mirror, I hear my husband's keys rattling.

"I'm in the car," he calls.

Only it isn't our car he is in, but our daughter's flashy yellow Mustang.

"So," I say, crawling in, "are we feeling a bit sporty tonight?"

"Yeah, why not?" he says, backing down the driveway. Despite his gray hair, he looks right at home behind the wheel.

At the restaurant, we are seated at a candlelit table, handed menus, and left to contemplate our appetites. This is one of our favorite places to eat. I already know what I want, so instead of studying the menu, I peer over the top of it and study the handsome man across the table.

In our years together, I have seen every expression he is capable of making, including the one he is wearing now—it is the what-to-order look.

"Can't decide?" I ask, almost certain he will end up with his usual prime rib.

"I thought about a steak," he says, "but prime rib sounds good, too."

The prime rib wins out, our order is taken, and we are left alone. We make small talk, then lapse into silence.

Marriage has a way of steadying nerves. Silence is okay. Tonight it gives me time to reflect.

People say that marriage has seasons. And it is true. We lived through seasons of barrenness and of plenty. Seasons when we couldn't stand to be apart, and seasons when we wondered how we stayed together.

But at this point in our marriage, we seem more settled than ever. We have nothing left to prove. We are comfortable together.

Does that mean we never argue?

No. But we know that a quarrel is not the end of the world, nor the end of a marriage.

Does that mean we lost the passion of our youth?

No. We still light each other's fire quite well.

Does that mean we evolved into perfect mates?

No. But we are two people who have accepted each other—warts and all. Two people who, despite their differences, plan to be together "till death do us part."

My husband reaches for my hand, pulling me from my musings. As I look into his eyes, I am filled with love for the man I married so many years ago, and I am deeply grateful that we chose to weather our many storms together, because tonight his eyes reflect nothing but love in return.

Dayle Allen Shockley

She Had His Heart

Love is a condition in which happiness of another person is essential to your own.

Robert Heinlein

"You look beautiful!"

She stared at her best friend's reflection in the mirror. Both women tried hard not to cry, not wanting to ruin their makeup. It had been a long journey. Rebecca knew the road her friend had traveled to get here—marked with potholes, dips of heartache, all leading toward this destination.

"Are you ready?" Rebecca asked, smiling.

"Yes," Anne whispered. "How does he look?" she asked, her voice quivering slightly with nervousness. "Does he look all right? Does he look nervous? Do you think he's okay?"

Rebecca tried to ease the worry she saw in her friend's deep brown eyes. She reached for Anne's hand.

How does he look? What could she say to her friend?

He wore a tuxedo. Or at least the shell of his body wore it.

He was eager. He was happy this day was here. She knew that from speaking to him earlier. His voice held the excitement of a child on Christmas morning preparing to unwrap that special gift. But he wasn't all right. In the past six months, the transformation of his body left us heartbroken.

His thick dark hair was gone—melted away by treatment. It wasn't that, though. His entire appearance was changed. His skin was pale, almost ghostly at times. No longer did his round face hold that glow of healthiness it once possessed. His sunken features caused him to look weathered. He'd lost so much weight. Every step his cancer-ridden body took registered with the pain that was a part of him. And as each month passed, leading to today, he grew weaker. Desperately he tried to keep his brave face on, not wanting to worry Anne. She was all he cared about, and this moment in time.

But time was not his friend.

"Beck?" Anne looked at her. Her friend's worry continued. "Is—he okay?"

Rebecca nodded. "He's in love! That's all that matters," she said. Her friend's face lit up once again with happiness.

"Oh! Did I show you what he sent to me this morning?" Anne crossed the room with excitement. She took each step with the bounce of a giddy schoolgirl. "It came with a dozen roses." Rebecca saw the flowers on the table near the corner of the room; they were a brilliant shade of red, clustered with simple elegance.

Rebecca admired Anne's strength. Anne stood poised in white lace and satin flowing down to the bottom of her train. Confidence glowed upon her face. Anne had finally found her hero.

But not all heroes are invincible. Hers was dying.

That didn't seem to matter now, though. Anne and Stathis were perfect for each other. They complemented each other like a pair of ripped jeans and old comfy sneakers—not perfect, but well matched when worn together. Jointly, they created a kind of harmony.

He slept more hours out of the day than most normal people. He was so tired from all the medications he was taking, simply to ease the pain his illness rendered upon him. When he was tired, Anne tucked him in.

When he was sick, Anne held his hand, telling him that every thing would be all right.

When he was stressed, Anne would make him laugh, which brought warmth to his face.

When his feet swelled up and he couldn't put on his shoes alone, Anne reached down, grabbing them to help him.

Every hospital visit and doctor's appointment, every arrangement that needed scheduling, she was there. Right by his side loving him.

They didn't go out much anymore. But neither were they waiting for him to die. They considered each precious moment that remained a miracle.

Rebecca worried for Anne's sanity when she and Stathis would be separated by death. What would Anne do? Rebecca swallowed the lump in her throat just thinking about it.

Then Anne handed her a card.

Rebecca opened it. Inside hung a long golden chain. Attached to it was half a golden heart.

The card read:

> *Inside this card you will find one piece of my heart.*
> *I want you to know when you're not with me, I feel torn apart.*
> *I have found comfort and peace in your arms, loving you this past year.*

*I am not saddened and my heart is content in knowing
the end is growing near.*

*Half of my heart belongs to me. The other half belongs
to you.*

*And when it's time for me to say good-bye. Just remem-
ber these words are true.*

*Together the pieces fit as we did, with a love that could
not be broken.*

*The friendship and trust you've given to me are such a
golden token.*

*For with you I had a reason to live when they told me I
was going to die.*

*And now and forever I will always be with you, for I am
ready to fly.*

*Please don't be sad or angry when it's time for you with-
out me to carry on.*

*Remember our love, hold on to our memories, and know
that you are strong.*

*I can't promise you today a life of forever. But together,
with you I'm not alone.*

*And after I'm gone the piece of my heart I'm wearing,
will find its way home.*

*I will wait for you as long as it takes to greet you when
it's time.*

*And forever know you own a piece of my heart on this
day you become mine.*

Stathis

Rebecca couldn't stop the tears from flowing as she read
the heartfelt words Stathis had written to Anne. She closed
the card, returning it to Anne's shaking hands.

"Would you help me put it on?" Anne asked, her tears
falling. Rebecca took the delicate necklace from her. She
attached the clasp and stepped back to look at her friend.

Her dress was gorgeous. Her hair was perfect. Right down to her shoes, Anne was an image of beauty. And with the golden necklace hanging around her neck, half a heart attached to it, Anne was going to be all right.

JP Shaw

7

THE POWER
OF GIVING

I've learned that people will forget what you said, people will forget what you did, but people will never forget how you made them feel.

Maya Angelou

His Trail of Love Notes

Marriage is the triumph of imagination over intelligence.

Oscar Wilde

"I love you. I love you. I love you," reads my love note as I caress it for the thousandth time. This love note is one of a trail of notes my beloved husband, my soul mate, planted before non-Hodgkin's lymphoma grabbed hold of his life.

Though my husband, Tony, had no great claim to fame or wealth, it was his gleaming smile and witty sense of humor that endeared him to others. His mantra was laughter, and it always sparked a smile or a chorus of laughter. His uplifting spirit, a remedy for my soul, blessed us throughout our marriage. But now that the laughter is gone, I take great comfort in his love notes—my medicine for living without him.

Two years ago, as my husband prepared for his passing, he painstakingly thought of me, how painful and lonely my life would be without him. My soul mate of forty-eight years mustered all of his strength to conquer his cancer, but as fate would have it, he succumbed to the inevitable.

Eight years prior to his own terminal illness, with God's grace, I survived my first bout of lung cancer. And he lovingly held my hand throughout my illness. Desperately holding on to hope, he prayed he'd beat his cancer as I had. He believed I held a sort of curative power that could heal him of his disease. So he'd rub my hand and pray with all his heart. But in both our minds, we knew cancer's cruel fate. Just the thought of me alone and without his comforting hand, without my beacon of light as I weathered the storm of multiple illnesses, pained him greatly.

My dear husband anticipated each minute detail I'd face without him—finances, home repairs, car maintenance, holidays, treatments and hospitalizations, birthdays, and our fiftieth wedding anniversary. How he must have envisioned me grappling with all these matters. So, like the nurturing gardener he truly was, he carefully planted a trail of love notes to guide me through the hills and valleys of life without him.

On the day of his passing, while sitting on my bed, I felt overwhelmed with images of my husband's last breath and his flickering gaze into my eyes; his medicine, prayer book, and tape recorder blurred on his nightstand.

I wiped away the tears and found the first of several love letters he left. Upon reading it, my teardrops blotched the letters and words of the parting message he had written for his beloved family and friends.

Accompanying his letter, my husband, also known as Pops, recorded an audio farewell tape. Sprinkled with humor and heartfelt gratitude, he thanked family and friends for all the fun-filled memories—family gatherings, holidays, football games, and family roasts. He even imaginatively inserted sound effects: a whistle on his farewell train, trailing off and vanishing into the clouds.

On the night of his passing, inside the drawer of his nightstand I found a love note that read: "To my beautiful wife. Thank you for all those wonderful years we had. Sorry I had to leave you. I will always love you. Take care, Mom."

How does one ever prepare for the loss of a soul mate? When does the endless numbness cease? For him, for me, I needed to carry on for our children and our grand-daughter. Each morning, I'd drag myself out of bed, and inch my way through yet another day without him. But when I'd least expect it, his loving presence awaited me as I'd stumble upon his trail of love notes.

One day while reaching inside my medicine cabinet, a daily routine I dreaded, I found another love note: "Mom, sorry I couldn't help take care of you when you had your knee surgery. Instead, you had to take care of me. You were so strong. You never complained. You were such a trooper. Always stay strong, Mom. You have the greatest determination. I love you."

Early the next morning while reaching inside the kitchen cupboard, yet another love note awaited me inside my coffee cup: "Hi, Mom! What a great cook you are. Thank you for all those great meals. You always took great care of me. Don't forget to give Denise your recipe for menudo and tamales. Keep that tradition alive during Christmastime." How I loved making his favorite dishes.

And in Cameron's playroom inside her favorite book, his love note to her read: "Cameron, you brought me so much joy. Sorry I had to leave you so soon. I love you."

Always an earnest provider, our family never went a day without our needs being met. One morning while retrieving a ten dollar bill, I found another one of his love notes: "Ah ha!" Don't take my money! Just kidding! Do what you'd like with it. You deserve it. Have a ball! I love you."

Sometimes I'd discover a love note in the most peculiar places, like the time I found a love note in the bathroom while opening a fresh box of toothpaste. His love note slid out. "Surprise! Hi, Mom! I miss you so much. Keep those choppers clean. Don't forget to get your teeth cleaned twice a year with Dr. Otto. Take care, my love. I love you." Or the time I found one inside my makeup bag. "I want you to take good care of yourself. You are so beautiful, Mom. I love you." The thrill he must have felt planting his love notes. I still see his gleaming smile and hear his familiar laughter.

Pops always paid close attention to important matters. On a new 2005 calendar, he flagged important dates for me to remember. February 15, 2005: "Don't forget your appointment with our tax man." February 20: "Remember to schedule your physical checkup. I love you."

And a few months later, when I finally decided to install hardwood floors throughout the house, my son found a love note hidden beneath the carpet in the corner of my bedroom. "Wow! You've finally decided to do it! Whatever you choose, wood or carpet, you've always been a great decorator. I know it will look nice. If it is carpet, fine, but please put hardwood floors in our bedroom. It can help stem your allergies. You'll always be the love of my life."

My wonderful husband took meticulous care of our cars, making sure they operated in tip-top condition. So when the unexpected happened, a lodged nail in my tire, I took my car in for service. In the corner of the trunk, the attendant found a bag of lug nuts. When he looked inside, he retrieved a love note for me: "I'm so sorry I had to leave you with all these decisions. If you decide to sell this car, you can give these lug nuts to the new owner, or keep them for a new car you most deserve. As always, I love you."

Anticipating my senior moments, my husband thought of times when I'd misplace my house keys: "Ah ha!

Someone lost their house key! Here's a spare key for you. I love you."

And while rummaging through my miscellaneous drawer, I found a crossword puzzle book with a note that said: "Promise me you'll keep your mind alert with these crossword puzzles. They will help you pass the time away. I'll love you forever."

My husband left no rock unturned. In fact, he made it a point to alert our Realtor, investor, and mechanic, individuals whom he trusted, to help me when I'd come knocking on their doors. A love note read: "I spoke with our Realtor about selling our property. Just call him. He'll already know how he can assist you." "Your car is due for an oil change and a tire rotation. You can trust our mechanic."

Inside a sugar bowl on our dinette, where we'd cozily talk and laugh for hours on end, he left me a love note that simply expressed: "I love you. I love you. I love you." I've held it so often it's weathered from my touch.

Only the four walls of my bedroom really know how desperately I've missed him. A couple of months after my husband's passing, my friend Pat convinced me to accompany her to Laughlin, Nevada, the excursion my husband and I enjoyed. Feeling a bit ambivalent, something tugged at me to accept her invitation. When I reached into our "special envelope," the one we customarily earmarked solely for this indulgance, to my surprise, another love note, along with a wad of bills secured by a paperclip, fell out: "Get away for a while, Mom. Have a ball! Enjoy yourself. I'll be there with you in spirit. Have a great time! I love you so much." Oddly, the casino ambiance and the familiar chiming and clanging of slot machines felt strange without him.

My life, forever changed, now held on to precious memories of him, of his precious love notes. And so as I wept in silence each night, hugging his soft pillow and smelling the scent of his cologne on it, I'd close my eyes and imagine his gleaming smile and the sound of his infectious laughter. His presence seemed so real and vivid I'd bathe myself in his presence before it faded away.

On one such night as I held his pillow to my bosom, a burst of wind blew through the sliding glass door and startled me. Strangely, it summoned me to open the bottom drawer of his nightstand. Hidden toward the front of the drawer was another love note, carefully folded and begging me to read it: "So sorry. I probably won't be here for your birthday. Just in case I'm not here, happy birthday. Have a great birthday. I love you so much."

Had he survived cancer, we'd have celebrated our golden wedding anniversary, I thought to myself. Deep in thought, another gale blew into my bedroom, this time knocking a CD onto the floor. Again I searched inside this same drawer and discovered another precious love note: "My beautiful wife, in our closet I've saved a special anniversary gift, especially for you. Open it on our fiftieth wedding anniversary. I'll love you forever."

"And I will forever love you, Pops."

As instructed, on our golden wedding anniversary, behind my shoe box on the top shelf of our closet, I found his lovely parting gift. Upon lifting the lid off the gift box, I suddenly gasped. A diamond-covered gold bar suspended on a gold necklace glistened like a cluster of stars. Tears welled up in my eyes as I held it close to my bosom and gently caressed it. His gift was the same necklace he had given to me on our silver wedding anniversary! Lost after so many years, he must have found it, restored it, and saved it for this special day. His love note beside the necklace read: "My dear wife, I'll forever love you. Throughout our marriage you made me so happy. I've always told everybody I hit the jackpot when I married you. If I could pluck each rose that expressed how much I love you, I'd walk forever in a rose garden. Emma, my beautiful wife; I love you with all my heart."

His love notes, as priceless as his gleaming smile and thunderous laughter, sustain my every waking moment. Now my husband's love notes spark in me a smile and a faint giggle I thought had withered away.

On my nightstand, inside a golden box, I keep my cherished love notes, the nourishment for my soul. And on his nightstand, next to his photo, my love note to him simply expresses, "I love you. I love you. I love you. Still you are my everything, Pops, until the day I board that farewell train with you. *Te quiero mucho.*"

Love,
Emma

Sandra Nevarez

A Space of Her Own

I put an apple in my pocket, clamped a book between my teeth, and scampered up the towering tree like a spider monkey. Then settling into the comfortable tree crotch that fit my child-size body like a recliner, I buried myself in the vinelike branches to lose myself in the lazy summer afternoon.

Years later, married, I tried to capture the essence as I told my husband, Norm, about my willow tree. It was my very own safe haven from a world not always kind. It is essential for everyone, not only children, to have a space and time to ourselves, where we can commune with nature, connect with the source of all things, and find our own voices. That willow was my sacred spot.

Shortly after Norm retired, we set out to live a dream I had envisioned all my life: to open a medical clinic in a third-world country. Life was simple in the rainforest of Belize and in sync with the rhythms of nature. We rose when the sun came up; we slept when it went down; in between we worked like Trojans to turn a corner of a dilapidated old building into a clinic.

On market day the buses came from distance villages. The women, up before dawn, needed to catch the bus into town to come to the clinic. The tiny Mayan women, who wore a bright rainbow of traditional dress, were already waiting when I arrived in the morning.

Sometimes it was difficult for me to understand the women. They spoke English, but it wasn't my English. I spent much time repeating questions and wondering if my patient understood them and if I could decode her answers.

To announce the opening of the clinic, I went to the local radio station, Wamalalie FM 105. *Wamalalie* means "our voice" in one of the local languages. I was thankful to announce our opening on radio instead of on television. I was having a bad hair day; no, I was having a bad hair year! A way-too-tight perm plus the scorching Belizean sun left me with curls that seemed to spring from my head, like wiry coils, in all directions. My husband, Norm, started calling me his "Wamalalie Mama." (I thought it endearing and began signing all notes I left him with my new signature, and to mock my new hairdo, I added a drawing of a simple smiley face with corkscrew hair springing out all around the head.)

Living in the rainforest of Belize recaptured the essence of my childhood willow tree. Even before the sun rose in the morning, I awoke to the hallelujah chorus of songbirds greeting the day. Thousand-legged centipedes invited close inspection as they inched their way across the floor. I attended to patients in the clinic while geckos scampered up the walls and termites built mud tunnels on the ceiling.

With few outside distractions, only one radio, no television, and no social commitments to fulfill, life went on at a lovely, unhurried pace. I rediscovered books and found myself reading with the complete abandon of my childhood.

But all too soon our time passed. We needed to return to our Midwestern lives. Sadly we said good-bye to the rainforest and to our new rainforest friends. I was reminded of a plaque my sister once gave me: *"It's hard to go back to Kansas once you've been to Oz."* How true it was!

I missed Belize. I missed the simplicity. I missed waking up to the cacophony of birdcalls and roosters. I missed the sight of a towering fan palm swaying in the breeze and the brilliant red sunrises that would take my breath away. I missed time to simply be or to read or write at an unhurried pace. I even missed the bugs! Those horrible, crawling, flying, stinging, and biting creatures made my life miserable yet, at the same time, were fascinating subjects in the lessons of nature.

I lamented to Norm how I wished for a little piece of nature of my very own and a place to lose myself in my reading and writing. I wanted a space where I could read a book, write a story, or simply be alone with my thoughts. In short, I wanted to climb high up in a willow tree and savor each lazy summer day.

"So this will be a 'No Boys Allowed' kind of place?" Norm quipped, with a grin.

"You've got the idea," I replied.

He set about building just such a spot for me. With no willow tree in our yard large enough, he chose a lofty maple tree. Right here, in the center of the Heartland, he built an awesome towering tree house that soars thirty feet in the air, complete with a swinging rope and wood bridge leading to it from the roof of the upstairs story of our house.

Once the project was complete, I began spending every free moment high in the tree house. Sometimes I simply lay in my treetop hammock and watched the ants march down a limb beside my head, or closed my eyes and let my ears fill with the piercing trill of the cicada's concert. I dragged a small table and a chair up and wrote stories of Belize, capturing my memories of the women there.

"I've one more thing to make for your tree house," Norm announced mysteriously one morning. I couldn't imagine what, but soon I heard the sounds of work coming from his shop—the buzzing of his saw, the high pitch whine of a router, and country music blaring on the radio.

Later, I heard a loud pounding in the backyard. I went to the door to see what it was. There was Norm high up in the air, just below the swinging bridge that leads to the tree house. He was nailing a sign to the outside of the protective railing that surrounds the deck. The sign read: NO BOYS ALLOWED! in large, bold letters, and under the words, a simple drawing of a smiley face with corkscrew hair springing out all around the head.

So Wamalalie Mama now has a space, "a room of my own," so to speak. And on any given sunlit day, if you look closely between the branches, you will find me, and my muse, high above the ground in a towering maple tree, blessed amid the birds and the bees . . . and the bugs.

Nancy Harless

A Love Story About a Ring

Where there is great love, there are always miracles.

Willa Cather

What is it about estate jewelry that captures us? I think part of it is the intimate connection we feel in having something touch our skin that long ago touched someone else's.

We picture the slender ruby necklace resting on young sunburned, freckled skin. We see the simple strand of elegant pearls on a youthful wrist that waits to know much of life. And the cameo brooch, so big, that laid against silvery silk on a grandmother's breast as she attended her granddaughter's wedding, seizing one last celebration of life while wearing the dress she loved.

I think of these never-to-be-duplicated moments when I hold a piece of treasured jewelry. I hope that someday, far away from today, somebody will pick up my favorite ring, look at it closely, feel the love I feel for it, and especially . . . feel a connection to me.

Shortly before our last anniversary, my husband, Bob,

said, "Now that we've been married for twenty-two years, it's time you had a diamond engagement ring."

I looked down at my simple gold wedding band. "But I love this ring."

"I know. But it would mean something to me to get you a diamond ring."

"We don't have the money for that."

"I've been saving."

Again, I looked at my lovely wedding band, remembering how Bob had presented it to me. A little over twenty-three years ago, we were having dinner at a fancy restaurant. I don't remember the main part of my entree, but I do recall it was covered with asparagus, cream sauce, and lobster. I can still see us: Bob in a gray pin-striped suit and me wearing a real piece of history—a black dress in a size five.

For dessert, we ordered napoleons. We held hands, both of us tired from the wine. The waiter brought our dessert on a silver platter. Next to my pastry was a tiny box, gift-wrapped in gold with a sparkly bow in the shape of a star. The waiter put our desserts on the table and then, in a grand gesture, presented me with the little box.

"What is this?" I can still feel the sting of those tears in my eyes. And I opened it to find the beautiful, tiny, antique gold wedding band I've now worn for twenty-two years.

And so, we held hands while we talked about Bob's wish for a diamond for me. And it was with tremendous guilt that I finally agreed to at least look at engagement rings.

It felt deliciously forbidding shopping for a diamond ring. We went through nearly all of the local antique shops, looking at old jewelry. And then I found it—a magnificent ring with historical richness of worn platinum filigree. On the card was the first name of its original owner, Etta, and it was dated in the late 1800s. I tried it on. It fit perfectly. Bob's eyes lit up when he saw how I looked at it so passionately.

I turned my hand this way and that, the aged-diamond sparkling under the lights. I wondered what Etta felt when she first put it on. Was she thrilled? Did she wear it every day until she died? Did she worry about losing it when she was doing laundry or digging in the sand with her children?

The masterpiece workmanship dazzled me. I fell in love with it. But, no, I couldn't buy it. Too frivolous. Who buys themselves a diamond ring, for heaven's sake?

That night over dinner, Bob said, "It looked wonderful on you."

"Well, have you looked at the 'bills to be paid' file lately?"

"You take something away from me by not treating yourself," he said later while we did the dishes.

I dreamed about the ring that night. In my dream, the ring was in a fire and the platinum was gone forever. I searched through the ashes for the diamond but never found it.

The next morning, I found Bob weeding the front garden. "I've been thinking about the ring," I said. "I really do love it." He stopped pulling up old thistle. "Let's just do it," I said. And he joyously came into the house to change before we drove back to the antique shop.

In the store's parking lot, he held up our checkbook, grinned like a kid, and said, "I'm ready!"

I felt so naughty rushing to the glass display case, and with the excitement of a child at Christmas, I looked for the ring.

It was gone.

"There was an old platinum ring here yesterday," I said to the saleswoman. She helped me search through the jewelry cases. Then she confirmed it wasn't there. She called over to a woman behind another counter who said, "We sold it yesterday."

"I can't believe it," my salesperson said. "It's been here for months." Then she gently admonished me. "Whenever you see something you like in an antique shop, you should take it. At least you could have told me you were interested, and I'd have held it for you for a little bit. But you didn't look like you really wanted it."

On the ride home, I felt bad for Bob, since he was obviously disappointed for me. "It's just a ring, sweetheart," I said. "There will be others."

"But we've seen over a hundred. And that was the one for you."

I'm embarrassed to say that I felt bad, too. There was just something about that ring.

I was in the throes of a head cold on the day of our recent anniversary, so we stayed home. Bob cooked mussels, clams, shrimp, and scallops in a wine sauce served over angel hair pasta. I didn't feel like setting the table with the lace tablecloth I had kept from my mother's estate. And I didn't feel like finding the matching napkins. I just felt too crummy from the cold. But I forced myself to do it for Bob, who gets enormous gratification, as I do, when we have intimate celebrations. He outdid himself all day wrestling with phyllo dough to make napoleons. However, they came out looking like globs of white mush.

I was blowing my nose and looking rather dreadful in my faded chenille bathrobe, when Bob brought the desserts to the table on a silver platter. There, next to mine, was a little gold box, gift-wrapped with a bow in the shape of a star.

"What is this?" With luscious anticipation, I wondered what beautiful ring my husband had picked out for me and, of course, I began to cry. I opened the tiny box.

Inside sat Etta's ring.

"But it was sold," I looked up at him, my eyes wide.

He was beaming. "I know. I went right back and bought it that first day."

"So the people there were acting?"

"Yes. We all were."

We both received timeless gifts that night. Twenty-two years of a love-filled blessed marriage and the exquisite tenderness that comes along with giving and receiving a gift from the heart.

And so, what once touched Etta's skin is now touching mine. I am hoping somehow she knows that a small part of her is bringing me great joy and that someday someone will want to continue the trail of love with this enchanting piece of jewelry.

But most important for now . . . I really want her to know . . . her resplendent engagement ring is safe and sound with me.

Saralee Perel

Presents of Mine

As the holiday approaches, my thoughts turn to the wonderful gifts my husband, John, might shower on me. I guess it is true, as they say, that hope springs eternal.

When I dated John, he was such a romantic guy. He wrote me tons of love letters and composed songs for me. He was a cadet at the United States Military Academy during our courtship, and on the weekends, John would spirit me to an isolated floor of Eisenhower Hall and serenade me with his guitar.

On my nineteenth birthday, John strolled me down the academy's Flirtation Walk along the Hudson River. He sat me on a wrought iron bench, dropped to one knee, and proposed. He presented me with a sparkling pear-shaped diamond ring. After I joyfully accepted and expressed my deepest feelings for him, I whipped out my jeweler's loop and studied the gem. I thought, *Now, this is a man who knows how to shop for me.* The warning buoy sounded on the river.

We spent our first Christmas as a married couple in Colorado Springs, Colorado. For months, I had saved and planned to buy John the perfect holiday gift. He worked long hours as a second lieutenant in the field artillery, including many weeks downrange on maneuvers. He needed to relax when he was home, so I bought him a plush recliner and a stereo system. On Christmas Eve, John returned home toting a huge meticulously wrapped present. I couldn't imagine its contents.

Christmas morning arrived, and as John lounged in his new chair, we opened the gifts from relatives and friends. He insisted that I save his gift for last. My hands shook with excitement as I tore the paper and revealed an enormous Crock-Pot. Let me mention here, that longtime friends and even those fellow shoppers who glance into my grocery cart filled with boxes of macaroni and cheese and Entenmann's desserts know that I don't cook. My idea of a special meal for cherished guests is overcooked spaghetti topped with warmed Ragu sauce, which one pal refers to as "magnetti" because of its sticking power.

I smiled as it slowly dawned on me that this was my husband's idea of a good-natured joke. He must have hidden something spectacular in this cavernous appliance. I dumped the Crock-Pot to the floor, dived into it, and searched it like an expert spelunker. The only treasures I unearthed were warranty information and a recipe pamphlet.

Over these last twenty years, I have amassed quite a collection of "John gifts": umbrellas, telephones, and computer accessories. Eek! Another mouse. My father, a clinical psychologist, tried to soothe me by analyzing the possible subconscious thoughts behind my husband's presents. "The umbrellas," Dad explained, "mean that John wants to protect you, and the telephones symbolize his wish to keep the lines of communication open."

I countered, "Maybe he thinks our relationship is stormy, and he wants to hang it up."

Last Christmas, I decided that subtle gift hints were hopeless. I found a breathtaking tanzanite and diamond ring at an exclusive Poughkeepsie jewelry shop. I attached a color picture of the ring, along with the jeweler's business card, the item number, and price, to the freezer with a magnet. On my husband's frequent power walks to the fridge for ice cream, he was certain to spot my annotated wish list.

I was giddy with anticipation when the holiday came upon us. John handed me yet another large container. I grinned. I had seen this trick in chick flicks, where the little ring box is concealed in a group of larger cartons to throw the receiver off track. I unwrapped the first box, and it said Super Armitron. I looked inside, and it was indeed a Super Armitron, a robotic arm toy. The accompanying note was a gentle jab at my lack of housekeeping skills. It read: To give you a hand around the house.

Finally, I realized that John's presence in my life is the greatest gift of all. However, this holiday season, I'll be driving to a particular jewelry store with the Super Armitron riding shotgun. I'll need its robotic strength to lift all that carat weight.

Marie-Therese Miller

Reprinted by permission of Off the Mark and Mark Parisi. © 2003 Mark Parisi.

Piano Love

What is a soul? It's like electricity—we don't know what it is, but it's a force that can light a room.

Ray Charles

A warm night breeze drifts through an open window as I sit at the piano. My fingers touch the keys and music swells to fill the room. The soft ballad I play comes from a place located deep within my soul. Melody floats out the window into the night to serenade a bird, a rabbit, or an occasional neighbor walking his dog. I am an anonymous musician sharing her deepest feelings with the world. This is my favorite time of day to play the piano.

During my teenage years, evening piano playing rescued me from kitchen duty. Mother loved to hear my music. When dinner ended, I would rush to the piano straight from the table and begin to play.

"Oh, that was so beautiful. Please, don't stop playing," Mother would say.

One song followed another. I didn't mean to avoid my

chores. But I would lose myself in the songs, not realizing the passing of time. Soon, the dishes were washed and it was too late to offer any help.

But it meant more than just music to me. The piano was my therapy. I played happily, bouncing from one song to another. I played when troubled. Oftentimes, my fingers traveled the keys while my mind drifted, and sometimes I pounded the keys until I had solved a niggling problem.

When I married, my piano playing ended. We did not own a piano for fifteen years. Then I learned of a neighbor who wanted to sell hers. I watched excitedly when my husband tied the piano to the back of a pickup truck and rolled it up the street to our driveway. The rickety legs and blurred sound that resulted from such an unorthodox journey did not dampen my joy.

At the time, my children were sick with chickenpox. I had no music except for the few sheets that remained in the bench of my newly purchased piano. Although the pieces were too easy, I played for hours, catching up on fifteen years of missed piano therapy.

Finally, I bought new music and my nightly serenades began again. I played with all my heart to the phantom audience that existed in the dark, outside of our house. But I missed Mother's appreciation of my music. For my husband couldn't hear the feelings or see the beauty in the notes I played each night.

Then I stopped playing the piano. I would sit down to begin, but the notes sounded wooden, and I had lost interest. The feelings weren't there and the music wouldn't come. I closed my soul to everything I loved, including my piano. I think I feared where my music might take me or what it might let me see. The birds and rabbits waited outside my window for their nightly serenade, only to hear the quiet of the night.

When I left my marriage, the piano came with me, and

slowly I began to play again. Then I serenaded the neighbors in my condominium building. They showed their appreciation by turning their TV volumes up to compete with my pounding piano therapy.

I restarted my life and met someone. We began the process of learning about each other.

"Did you say that you play the piano?" he asked. "Would you play sometime for me? I love to hear a good piano."

My heart skipped a beat. I happily played piano that night. The neighbors turned up their TVs even louder.

One day after playing for him, he looked at me and said, "You deserve to play your music on a special piano. After we are married, I promise to buy you a grand piano. And I always keep my promises."

The soft desert light fades to evening. I sit behind a gleaming mahogany grand piano and begin to play. The soulful sound permeates the room. Music swells then softly ends.

"Honey, that was beautiful," he says. "Will you please play it again for me?"

Donna L. Hull

8

SPECIAL MOMENTS

The heart has its reasons which reason knows not of.

Blaise Pascal

When the Heart Speaks

We lived on a small farm in Campobello, with rolling pastures and streams that cut through the beautiful hardwoods and pines. The views of the mountains makes ones heart sing.

Our family of eight, with four girls and two boys, loved to play on this beautiful land. My mother worked hard to cook, clean, and sew for us. She always took time to share her love of nature, art, music, and books with us. My father also worked hard on the land and taught school.

On a spring morning, the sun shone on the green pastures; the wildflowers were in full bloom. Mother, with six small children, had so much work to do that lovely Saturday she could not leave the house, but dreamed of crossing the green pastures to the edge of the wood to see the flowering trailing arbutus. Mother almost felt resentful that she could not get out and explore the lovely wildflowers.

Dad, as always, was in the fields hard at work, wearing his usual work clothes and his old green felt hat.

Lunchtime came around and dad returned from the fields; Mother looked out the door while he crossed the bright green pastures. The sunlight beamed down on him and Mother could see he was carrying something in his hands. She stepped onto the porch for a better view. As he came closer, Mother watched the sunlight dance on the beautiful soft pink flower bouquet of trailing arbutus spilling out of his old green felt hat and falling over his strong hands. Dad knew what Mother was thinking and feeling that beautiful spring day.

When the heart speaks.

Julia Burnett

The Last Dance

Everyone is the age of their heart.

Guatemalan Proverb

I waited for the nurse to dress Mom after her shower. She had lived in a nursing home for a year. It was a pleasant environment and Mom actually liked it. Since Dad had passed away, she craved the closeness of family and friends and joined in every seniors' activity group in our area. When she fell and broke her hip at age eighty-nine, she didn't heal well from the replacement surgery and wound up first in a rehabilitation facility and then in a permanent nursing home that provided her with the medical attention and twenty-four-hour care she needed.

The facility met not only her medical, but also her social needs. She quickly made several friends in the home, and constant activities kept her busy and entertained. The people who ran the nursing home were, in general, very nice. The rooms were as pretty as possible considering the beds were, out of necessity, hospital style. But the gardens, outdoor patios, and the several different recreation rooms compensated for the hospital beds. The home scheduled regular card games and movies and even a provided a beauty salon. I spent one full day with Mom every week, and it seemed that somebody always celebrated a birthday party, complete with entertainers.

That night, the regular monthly starlight dinner was planned for all who wanted to attend, with a "piano man" and floor space for dancing—for those who could still dance. Tables were spread over one of the large outdoor patios to mimic a real nightclub, and the orderlies wore waiter and waitress apparel.

After we came back from the in-house beauty salon, I helped Mom select an outfit for the event. She was almost as giddy as a teenage girl getting ready for her prom. Even though confined to a wheelchair, she was looking forward to the dance.

"Friday is special," she said with a dreamy look on her face. "You remember, don't you?"

"Sure, Mom," I replied. How could I ever forget? Rain or shine, sickness or strife, the whole time we were growing up, Mom and Dad "dated" on Friday nights. They would go out to dinner and dancing. If one or the other was ill, they made an evening of it by turning on the stereo, playing big band music, and dining by candlelight in the living room, complete with some bubbly.

They worked hard at their small business all week, and the Friday night tradition was a reward for them.

As we grew up, left home, married, produced grandchildren, and they, in turn, produced great-grandchildren, Mom and Dad never wavered from this tradition. Even when Dad's Parkinson's became so bad that he could hardly walk, Mom helped him get spruced up and they would go out, even if only to the little piano bar around the corner from their apartment.

When Dad passed away, Mom threw herself into

volunteer work and activities at senior clubs. She became a one-woman welcome wagon, traveling around entertaining at various affairs by playing the piano and singing. But Friday nights were lonely. I always tried to visit or at least call, but it wasn't the same. Throughout their sixty-year marriage, Mom and Dad had always enjoyed their special night and now it was gone.

The residents of the nursing home were invited to ask family members to come to the dinner dance, so I asked Mom if she would like me to come back that evening. Surprisingly, she said, "No."

"I don't think you need to bother. You're busy and need to take care of your own life. Don't worry about me. I'll be fine," she said. She was adamant. I could tell she really did want to do this alone.

"Are you meeting a boyfriend?" I asked, teasing her.

Her hazel eyes twinkled, and a sly grin spread over her face. "That's for me to know and you to guess." She patted her newly curled hair and asked to see my compact. While she preened in the small mirror, I wondered if it could be true.

There were a lot of nice looking elderly gentlemen in the home, so it was a possibility. However, Mom had never given anyone a second look since Dad died, so this was unusual. "He was my one and only," she often said. "Your father was the love of my life and nobody could ever replace him."

I helped her dress in a nice evening outfit before I left that day. She was eager for me to leave and kept asking me if I had work to get back to. She basically hustled me out the door. I made a promise to myself to come back on Saturday to see if she would let me in on the fuss from the previous night. I left finally, my head spinning with questions.

In the middle of the night, the phone rang; it was the nursing home. Mom passed away in her sleep. When they conducted their regular eleven o'clock bed check, the nurse had found her, lying peacefully in her bed, a photo of Dad resting under her hand at her chest, a smile on her face.

When I remember that day, I envision Mom sitting in her wheelchair, all dolled up and waving good-bye to me, her face flushed with anticipation of the evening to come. I like to think that her "date" was with Dad and that some- how she knew she would see him again that night. Maybe it's just hopeful thinking, but when I remember her sly smile and the sparkle in her eye, I do believe that Dad, the love of her life, did come back to her that night and took her away with him for their final Friday night dinner dance—one that will last for eternity.

Joyce Laird

Magical Moments at the Old Yard Swing: Inspired by Love and a Broken Heart

There is no pain so great as the memory of joy in present grief.

Source Unknown

Estelle, I love you. I want to hold you tight and kiss you once again and dance the dance you loved so much. Free from Earth's bounds, Estelle. I know we can't—but in my dreams I pray that we could. But I know in this life it shall not happen except in my dreams.

Every time I walk in our front yard, I see that old porch swing hanging from the pine tree, and I think of you and the day you brought it home from a yard sale, so proud that you had paid only $10.00. Then you sanded it down and put several coats of varnish on it. Until the day I die, I will remember all the good times we had on that old yard swing.

Now, in the spring, as your flowers come alive, I will sit there alone on your favorite swing by the stream in our front yard just thinking. I will listen, and when I hear the warm and gentle breeze whisper through the pines, I will think of you, and I will think that you have come to visit me. And as I feel the soft and warm wind upon my face and listen to it whispering its secrets to me, let me feel the gentle touch of your hand upon my hand, so that I will know you are there sitting next to me. Then I shall feel warm, and we will think of things that were and things that could have been. And we will sit there together for a while, you and I, in the warm spring air among the blooms of the beautiful flowers and gardens of your yard that you loved so much.

We will share memories from the past: of our grandchildren playing in the stream, the Easter egg hunts, the fun they had shaking the fur off the cattails, all the fun we had making it all happen, and all the other wonderful things memories are made of. So when you see me there alone on that old yard-sale swing with the varnish peeling off and hanging from the pine tree, come and gently give my hand a touch so that I know you are there sitting with me and have forgiven me for the things I didn't see and didn't do.

Then we shall talk and talk and flirt and flirt and be in love as only you and I can be. And in that magical moment may we feel each other strong enough and the music of the wind blowing through the pine trees will be real enough that we take each other in our arms and dance our favorite dance around our yard of beauty and memories. Then maybe for a few moments, just a few, I will feel your embrace, the rhythm of your body, hear your breath, smell your sweet perfume, caress your face, squeeze you tight, and feel you move closer. I whisper in your ear, "I love you." And you hear me! And I hear you say, "Yes, I know, dear." And may that magical moment relieve some of the pain in my heart.

And as time goes by and the family gathers here and the

children and grandchildren are laughing and playing in the yard, I will always go alone to that old swing in the yard and wait to feel the gentle touch of your hand upon mine, and I will sit there peacefully for a while, knowing that you are there with me as you would have been in life, enjoying our family and home together.

"Estelle, until the next magical moment of dance, I await your gentle touch."

R. Goulet

Vegetable or Fruit?

Cheju Island, Korea

My jet-black-haired, red-cheeked wife, Mi-Ra, stooped before our tiny table. I moved past her and toward our tiled hallway. But a glimmer in her eyes shone. Something was up. I cast my glance out the window. I was starting to learn. Directness accomplished little here. Whatever had nurtured her grin would reveal itself . . . eventually.

Frost on the edges of our sliding paper-waxed window reminded me that we were still in the middle of a Korean winter. Not that I had forgotten; I never felt so cold. A glance through the clear, unfrosted center of the window revealed more proof that Korea was a land of surprises and contrasts. In the far distance, the mountain peaks lay capped in snow. Yet, a few steps from the doorway, our modest one-room house sat in the midst of a fruiting orange grove. I knelt at our knee-high faux mother-of-pearl table. Mi-Ra presented me with a bowl. The smile returned.

"Wow, incredible. Where'd you get it?" I asked, peering into the bowl.

"The U.S. military base."

My jaw dropped, "You went all the way to the other side of the island and somehow got on the U.S. military base to get Cocoa Puffs for me?"

"Yes."

"I think I should keep you," I joked.

"Yes."

Food was a major problem for me. Kimchee, that rough, fermented, garlic-infested cabbage, was certainly made with an eye to longevity and preservation, but it hadn't been made with me in mind. Just last week I'd had a dose of food poisoning so evil I could barely crawl to our stone-lined outhouse. When I managed to struggle back to our house, I just lay on the tile-lined floor, grabbing my gut.

So . . . Cocoa Puffs in the morning was an unparalleled treat.

"And what is this?" I added as I detected small shiny red objects hidden beneath the cereal.

"Fruit," Mi-Ra said with pride. She poured milk in. Real milk, not soy milk.

I had decided on my second day on Cheju Island that I would keep her . . . if she let me. I said it again, "I think I better keep you. Wow! Cherries. Where did you get cherries?"

"Close your eyes," she requested, with a happy sparkle.

I complied. My brain sent an electronic message to the receptors in my tongue. The message—*cherries*! Sweet cherries! Get ready for the crunchy texture. Be careful of the hard pit. God, cherries! Mi-Ra shoveled in a hefty spoonful and laughed. I bit down and my brain went haywire. The cherry exploded with soft mushiness. I spit it into my hand.

"What the heck is it?" I asked, wiping my mouth.

A look of horror crossed her face. "Fruit. You like fruit. I watched your foreign friends eat fruit in their cereal."

"What kind of fruit is it?"

"Tomato."

I laughed. "Tomato!"

She turned red. I loved it when she blushed. She hated it. She turned to face a wall. I heard her sniffle. I moved over to comfort her.

"What's up? It's cute. Cherry tomatoes instead of strawberries or cherries. So what. You tried and I am the only person on Cheju Island eating Cocoa Puffs. I'll keep you. I'll keep you."

And I did, or, rather, she kept me; for twenty-three years now we've eaten together, but I haven't had another bowl of Cocoa Puffs and tomatoes.

Paul H. Karrer

Gone with the Summer Breeze

*Love is never lost. If not reciprocated, it will flow
back and soften and purify the heart.*

Washington Irving

When you're a kid, a skinned knee feels like the end of
the world. A dropped ice cream cone is a disaster. And
when you think of someone not being around, it means
something like your best friend getting the chicken pox
and can't go to school for the annual Christmas party.

But as you grow older, your perception of a "catastrophe" begins to change. Those skinned knees turn into broken hearts, and dropped ice cream shifts into dropped
classes. There are times when you wish growing up didn't
take so long, and others when you want to go back to one
particular day and live in it for the rest of your life. You
make new friends, but never forget the old. You travel to
amazing places you've never seen before, but still have
that one special place you call home. You watch people
change, but you feel yourself stay the same.

And somewhere along the way you come to realize that

the past remains the past, that memories are not replaceable, and that leaving doesn't always mean coming back.

To most people, Eric was an average eighteen-year-old guy. He graduated high school, had a caring family, and loved to go bowling every Friday night with the guys.

To me, Eric was a hug at the end of a bad day. He had something special about him. Maybe it was that contagious smile that could light up the bottom of the ocean. Or the voice that gave me butterflies every time he whispered "I love you" in my ear. Whatever it was, he was the only one who could make me laugh until my belly went numb, and he always knew what to do to make me laugh when I didn't even want to smile.

No matter where we ventured, Eric and I made the best of every day. We rode water slides and screamed the whole way down. We challenged each other on upside-down roller coasters to see who could last the longest. Some days we preferred to just lounge around the house, watching movies and eating popcorn. Eric loved to surprise me with unexpected visits, bringing me my favorite ice cream, or random phone calls just to say good morning. There were nights when we stayed up for hours talking on the phone, knowing we'd see each other in the morning. We watched uncountable sunsets on our blanket in the grass, and we wouldn't get up until the sun disappeared and the moon shone like a spotlight on our cheeks. Sometimes I'd ask, "What do you see in us, Eric?"

"The world, Manda," would always be his reply.

He always carried big dreams. He wanted to travel the world and see all that it offered him. I remember the time that we hopped into the car and went driving, with no map and no plan, just to see where we would end up. When Eric told me he was joining the military, I knew there was no changing his mind. He needed to find his place.

I always knew the day would arrive when we would have to say good-bye. I guess I just avoided thinking about it, hoping I would wake up soon and realize it was all just a dream. A month turned into a week, and a week into three days. When the night came when he showed up at my door with my favorite yellow lilies and tears in his eyes, I knew the time had arrived.

We walked out to our favorite chairs at the back of the house, where we spent late nights and early mornings talking and laughing about anything in the world. But the weather cooled. Summer was ending, and so was our time together. We tried to picture what our lives would turn into. Where we would be and what we would look like when we saw each other again. But it was all just a hazy cloud of undetermined fate, like a wildflower seed floating through the summer breeze, just waiting to land, not knowing where or when.

I walked him outside like I always did when I didn't want him to leave. The words of that night still echo in my head: "If I never see you again to tell you this, please know that wherever I go and whatever I do I will love you for as long as I live."

I wanted to tell him to stay—that we could pack our bags and run away and never look back. "Never forget me," I whispered as he pulled me into his arms one last time. He didn't have to say he wouldn't. His hand against my face, wiping away my tears, said it all. The last thing I remember was watching his figure fade into the dark night. I stood there until I knew he was gone, but as I walked through the doorway, I turned around for one last glimpse. Once I realized there was nothing left but the cool fall night with its rustling trees and mysterious smell of falling leaves, I shut the door and locked it. I knew that this time he was gone for good. This was our last goodnight.

Sometimes in love, you need to let go. Maybe some

people aren't meant to stay in your life forever; some come and go, while others leave but remain a memory.

As more summers pass, the memory of Eric will never be replaced. Wherever he may live today, a part of him will always stay here with me. When the gentle wind of summer blows across my face, I can still smell the scent of him. I can almost feel his warm arms around me and his delicate hand running through my sun-kissed hair. It's on these days that we are together again. But I know that Eric is where he belongs.

Eric, to the world, was an acquaintance, a brother, a friend. Eric, to me, *was* the world.

Amanda English

Who's Kissing Whom Now?

I swear I was not spying. I just happened to be walking very quietly and looking around the corner when I saw them. They were sitting on the couch very close to each other, a little too close if you ask me. His arm was draped around her shoulders, and her head rested comfortably on his shoulder, a little too comfortably if you ask me.

I was just about to walk into the room and let them know that I was in their presence when it happened. She lifted her head and turned to face him at the same time he turned to look at her. I saw him lower his face, and I saw her raise hers. Oh, no! It was happening! Their lips were locking! They were kissing! This was terrible!

Ever so slowly, I tiptoed backward until I hit the stairway. Then I raced up the stairs and tore into the bedroom, slamming the door behind me. I had to tell him what I had just witnessed in our very own home!

"Oh, my gosh! You're never going to believe what I just saw!" I stammered breathlessly.

He barely looked up from the television.

"Did you hear me?" I practically shouted. "A travesty just occurred under this roof!"

Only then did he turn away from the screen and look at me. Obviously, travesties of this magnitude were of little concern to him. "What now?" he asked, with a yawn.

"They kissed!" I spat.

"They did what?" he asked, sitting up in the bed. Now I had his attention.

"I said they kissed!" My head fell into my hands. "This is awful!" I moaned. "It's too soon! I'm not ready for this!"

He patted my shoulder consolingly. "Do you think it's their first time?" he asked in an unsteady voice.

Now he had my attention. I looked up. "Of course, it's their first time—isn't it? Surely they haven't been carrying on like this right under our noses!"

"Well, they have been dating for a few weeks. I guess it's natural at their ages," he said slowly.

I jumped up from the bed and glared at him. "Don't you dare say that! There is nothing natural about this! This is . . . perfectly unnatural!" I could feel my temperature spiking and hear my decibel level rising. "Why, do you realize this is a public display of affection! This is PDA! That, my friend, would result in a suspension at school! This is . . . terrible!" I screeched.

Before he could answer, there was a knock at the door. "Mom? Dad? Are you okay?"

I looked at him and he looked at me. Had they heard us?

I slowly went to the door and turned the handle. There they were, our lovely teenage daughter and her handsome boyfriend! I smiled—sort of.

"Oh, we're fine, dear! That must have been the television," I said brightly, maybe a little too brightly.

"Um, okay, whatever," said our kissy-faced daughter as she held tightly to her beau's hand. "Well, Chris is fixing to leave, so I'm going to walk him out to his car to tell him 'bye. Be back in a few minutes!" she called casually as they bounced down the stairs, with the carefree steps of young people in love, young people like my husband and I had once been.

I looked at my husband. He gave me a wink and pulled me close. Maybe that one little kiss was not all that terrible, I thought as I snuggled in his arms—but I did mean that one little kiss!

"You know," I said dreamily to my husband as he held me in his arms, "they actually remind me of the two of us when we were that age."

"Yeah," he answered just as dreamily. "Remember how we were back then?"

"Oh, I do," I said with a smile.

At the exact moment, *those* memories became very vivid in both of our minds. We immediately separated and looked at each other with very wide eyes.

"You go out to that car and get her and bring her back in this house right now!" I squealed.

My husband was already down the stairs!

Terri Duncan

I Struck Gold

Emmitt, the prize "catch" of high school, was the all-state center, the track star, and so very tall, dark, and handsome. Needless to say, all the girls swooned over him. My popularity suffered big time with the females in our little country high school because Emmitt only had eyes for me.

The day after our high school graduation in May of 1945, Emmitt received his draft notice from Uncle Sam. We clung to each other and cried. I watched that big Greyhound bus carry my high school sweetheart away from me.

Emmitt wrote faithfully during those years. He told me how homesick he felt and of his love for me. Yet not one single time did he ever mention anything about marriage.

Finally, after what seemed to me to be an eternity, Emmitt's tenure in the army ended.

I counted the hours until I would see him. When I saw him get off the train, I gasped. The most handsome man in the world ran into my arms. My joy turned to disappointment and dismay, however, when he told me he and some army buddies were going to Alaska to strike gold. What a letdown! It made me mad! I hadn't planned to say it. In fact, I was shocked at what I heard coming out of my mouth: "Will you marry me?" I screamed.

Emmitt had the most surprised look on his face. Then he swooped me up in those big strong arms and said: "I thought you'd never ask."

On our wedding day, he took my hands in his and pledged all his love. After fifty years, Emmitt still holds my hands. Many times I awaken in the night and hear him whisper, "I love you."

Our three wonderful sons are tall, dark, and handsome too, just like their daddy. I've reached up to hug handsome men for a lifetime. Now I reach up to hug tall beautiful grandchildren. I feel those same familiar strong arms around me they inherited from their granddaddy.

Our marriage is interwoven with the gold Emmitt started out to discover.

We lived many disappointments and setbacks, but through our love for the Lord and for each other, we have been the recipients of many "golden moments."

Our children and grandchildren recently hosted a golden wedding anniversary celebration for us. The best part of the celebration was when Emmitt took me in his arms on our golden wedding night and whispered in my ear: "Remember when I came home from the army and was going to Alaska to strike gold? Well, instead, I stayed here and struck gold."

The real secret is, I am the one who struck gold!

Joan Clayton

My Johnny Angel

*While we try to teach our children about life,
our children teach us what life is all about.*

Angela Schwindt

Once in while you are lucky enough to find a special someone who makes a difference in your life. Out of the blue, I found that special someone, but fate wasn't about to give him to me so easily and decided to throw me a curve ball instead.

My sons, now fine young men, informed me not to move too fast on this relationship because I needed to get their approval first! They felt this was the right thing to do and pointed out that since I had looked after them prior to their manhood, it was now time to reverse the role. How does it come to pass that a mother lets this happen?

For a month I sat across the room, secretly watching him. He gave up his chair for the ladies, sported a great sense of humor, and helped anyone who needed it.

I tested the waters and accepted a date from this strange gentleman.

His aura made him very different; I wanted to solve the mystery.

We started out as friends and ended up falling in love.

He certainly convinced me; so now we needed to receive the "thumbs-up" from my male offspring—not an easy feat!

After living as a single mother for a few years, I thought I had finally gained my independence. Not so! I was suddenly hit with the realization that now I needed to answer to my babies! Something was very wrong with this picture.

For some reason, my sons formed a coalition against my expert decisions and decided that it really didn't matter whether I liked the idea or not. Pure mutiny if you asked me!

Although I had made a few wrong choices in my previous relationships, I felt they should trust my judgment; but they would hear nothing of it.

The interrogation begins . . .

It started as a friendly meeting at a local restaurant. They tried to do it discreetly, of course, slipping into the conversation questions, such as "And where do you work?" "How long have you been there?" "Have you ever been married before?" "Do you have any kids?"

John knew exactly what they were up to and did his best at feigning stupid. What surprised me the most was that it didn't even bother him! Once we were alone, he told me not to worry about the outcome of the evening. My sons were only doing what they thought was best for their mom, and he respected that.

He passed the test with flying colors. They saw in him exactly what I saw in him: a warm, genuine, caring soul.

We were married on October 6, 2001. My sons gave me away, and I knew they felt rather relieved that the burden no longer rested on their shoulders. They finally found someone brave enough to take me off their hands. Their philosophy: "It was a tough job, but somebody had to do it."

At the wedding, they literally did the high five in front of all the guests immediately after the minister pronounced us man and wife! The audience of more than 180 roared with laughter.

Surprisingly enough, marriage never changed my new husband as it does some men. He formed a strong bond between us by cementing our friendship with loyalty and kindness. I have yet to find a more dedicated family man. He is the epitome of the word *gentleman*.

And his quick wit and sense of humor always surprise me. One November evening shortly after we were married, I stood at the bathroom sink in my underwear, applying my makeup. We were getting ready to go out to a dinner and dance. John was just getting out of the shower when I heard him say behind me. "Mm, nice butt!"

Now I'm a fairly big woman and even though I can't see my butt, I know it's not all that great looking! "Are you talking to me?" I asked him.

"Well, honey," he replied, "I'm not standing here with a mirror behind my back."

This is my husband, the man I am destined to spend the rest of my life with. He is my best friend, my partner, my confidant.

He is, and always will be, my Johnny Angel.

Mary Ann Bennett-Olson

On Lunch and Love

But what minutes! Count them by sensation, and not by calendars, and each moment is a day.

Benjamin Disraeli

It is lunchtime. Twelve noon, on the dot. I hurry to prepare the usual meal: grilled ham and cheese for my husband, half a turkey sandwich on whole wheat (hold the mayo) for my calorie-conscious self. I chop a green apple into neat slices, then set out our centerpiece—a bowl of pretzels, a few potato chips.

The sound of the creaky garage door signals the arrival of my husband, home from work at his nearby office.

"My lunch had better be on the table!" he teases, then gives me a kiss. Laughing, I hand him his preferred drink, Cherry Pepsi, then sit down for my favorite hour of the day. It has been quite a morning—getting both of our girls off to school (Do you have your library books/lunch box/homework/extra shoes?), dashing off to the grocery store, and heading home to face several loads of laundry.

This time, a solid hour to sit down and reconnect with my spouse, is a welcome breather in my hectic life. I depend on it, and actually yearn to hear the rusty metal hinges on our garage opening, bringing my husband home each afternoon.

For a full hour we feast; filling ourselves not just with sandwiches and chips, but also with support and companionship. Crunching on apples, we commiserate about our mornings. "The computers were down, so things were really slow at the office. I just didn't accomplish all that much," he confesses.

"That's okay. I didn't even get to work on my writing today." Looking at the pile of laundry peering at me from around the corner, I wonder if the afternoon will be any different.

"Go get that piece you have been working on. You can read it to me."

So I read and he listens, offering a gentle suggestion here or there. "It is really good writing," he reassures me. "I like where it is going." Buoyed by his (mostly) truthful remarks, I am energized. Maybe I can find time to work on my story this afternoon.

We savor creamy raspberry yogurts and linger over our desserts before finally kissing good-bye. As his car backs out of the driveway, I wave, truly sorry to see him leave.

The next morning, I rush to leave a church meeting so I can make it home in time for lunch. My friends, of course, know what I am up to. They are suspect, maybe even jealous, of my routine. "Oh, I would hate to have my husband at home in the middle of the day!" they remark, rolling their eyes. "What a pain!" Smiling, I casually reply, "Oh, it isn't all that bad," before hurrying out the door, eager to fall into my husband's loving embrace.

We will meet again for lunch tomorrow and, God willing, for many tomorrows to come. Some days, we will feed our souls with talk of politics and current events. Other days, we will simply gossip and hold hands across the table like silly teenagers. The menu will vary, from bubbly tomato soup and grilled cheese in midwinter, to chicken salad and fresh strawberries come summertime. But the reassuring comfort of our routine, as dependable as the forward ticking of the clock, is a constant I will fight to protect.

The most beautiful sound in the world—the squeaky grinding of the garage door at noon—means everything to me. I will make the sandwiches and pour the Pepsi. Soon we will sit together again, filling up on love and laughter, refueling for the afternoon ahead.

Stefanie Wass

Stairway to Heaven

At fifteen, I first set eyes on him while at a high school basketball game with my best friend, Peggy. Folding chairs were set up on the stage to accommodate the large crowd. We sat down to watch the action.

With so many cool boys around, the game held little satisfaction for me. But I wasn't bored. Peggy cheered beside me. My gaze flicked over the team. When I finished checking out the boys on the court, I worked my way up the bleachers. Then as my eyes moved over the players on the bench, my heart flip-flopped in my chest.

Right there before me was the most beautiful guy I'd ever seen. He sprawled on the bleachers, a look of disgust on his face. It was obvious that he wanted to play in the game.

I couldn't breathe. Chills cascaded down my back, and I gripped my popcorn so hard that it spilled over the top of the bag. Time stood still. Sound stopped. My peripheral vision blurred until there was nothing left except this perfect place in the center where that amazing boy rested.

Dark, wavy hair brushed against wide shoulders. Thick, shaggy sideburns, and a generous amount of chest hair (be still my heart!) added to the perfection. When he smiled, my heart burst from sheer joy.

At that moment, the audience jumped to its feet and he disappeared. For a frantic instant, sound returned, and I glanced at Peggy's open mouth and flailing arms. A sadness pooled in my belly. Nothing happening on the court was as special as what I'd just glimpsed, but there was no way to explain it to her. Instead, I stood on tiptoe and peeked through the crowd, but to no avail. I could not find him in a sea of waving arms and squirming bodies. A moment later, everyone plunked back down.

I stood alone . . . spellbound.

"What are you doing?" Peggy whispered, aghast at my behavior. "Sit down," she hissed. I couldn't. The view was well worth any embarrassment it caused. She tugged again, this time more forcefully. "What are you doing?"

My arm rose of its own accord and pointed to the bleachers. "See that boy over there?" Peggy looked where I pointed. "I'm going to marry him." My comment met with a few chuckles and rolled eyes as those nearby judged me insane. I didn't care. Fireworks crackled in my head. I just knew we were meant for each other.

As I watched, he slumped forward, one elbow resting on his knees as he idly plucked at a shoelace. I sighed dramatically. He was what the word *hunk* described. At that moment, as if he felt the vibes my heart scattered across the gymnasium, he looked up. For a split second his attention was riveted on the stage. I wanted to shout to him, to say something . . . anything. But before I could react, the buzzer sounded, diverting his attention back to his teammates.

I twisted around and clutched Peggy's arm. "Oh, God. Did you see him look at me?"

She frowned and glanced around to make sure our conversation wasn't overheard. "He wasn't looking at you," she whispered. "He was watching the clock."

My heart plummeted to my feet. I could barely make it to the car with my trembling legs. Though emotionally exhausted, I managed to inquire about the boy with the dark, wavy hair. My sister, Ron, shot me a look that said it all. She knew him! His name was Tom.

I'll never forget the day his 1966 blue LeMans drove into our driveway for the first time. I sat in the living room, painting my toenails. I knew his car from the sound with my eyes closed. I nearly fainted. Ron and her friend, Cindy, however, knew how to control their emotions. Before I uttered a single word, the two stepped off the porch. Like a sleepwalker, I stumbled as far as the screen door.

"Hey, what's going on?" Ron asked, twirling a lock of naturally curly hair around her index finger skillfully. I watched speechless, learning what I could. My long straight hair never twisted as coyly, nor did I have the body language my sister displayed. How I wished I was her. The sound of the muffler rumbling and the melody of "Stairway to Heaven" spilled out the open window—well . . . it was heaven. I never wanted to be someone else so badly in my entire life.

Seconds before I offered up my soul for an instant of recognition in Tom's eyes, he looked straight at me just like he'd done the first time I saw him. His eyes quickly traveled across my face before he turned his attention back to my sister. Ron turned and waved me over. I clomped forward, the nail polish brush still gripped tightly in my right hand, one shoe on and one shoe off. Ron introduced me as her little sister.

I stood by speechless as Ron and Cindy climbed into the backseat. I stood there watching until the car disappeared from sight.

It was some weeks later before I saw him again, and by then, he and Cindy were inseparable. Oh, if only I was sixteen. Maybe he wouldn't have looked at Cindy at all! Still, a girl knows when a boy is interested, and I noticed Tom's covert glances.

Meanwhile, his best friend was sending looks my way. Duane and I had a lot of fun, but I think in his heart he knew I only wanted his best friend.

As the weeks flew past, I watched as Tom's relationship with Cindy began to crumble. I felt like a scumbag and distanced myself from Duane. Actually, I avoided Duane. I was young and in love and I couldn't help myself from acting like a creep, and I didn't have the words to explain myself. Tom would soon be free to love me. What choice did I have?

I apologized to Duane and set my sights on the boy with the dark, wavy hair. When it was finished between Tom and Cindy, I made my move. My initial impression in no way had changed. Tom was the boy I was going to marry, simple as that.

Once Tom finally asked me out, I never looked back. The song "Stairway to Heaven" became our song. When we danced, he held me close and changed the words just for me and sang, "Stairway to Helen's." To this day that phrase can turn me to mush.

We were going steady before the year was over and walked down the aisle two years later. Much to my delight, we've spiraled higher yet with the births of our three children.

It's not every day my heart thumps as wildly as it did that magical evening in a crowded gymnasium some thirty years ago, but we are still in love and "Stairway to Heaven" is still our song. We even own a jukebox in our entryway to remind us of our wonderful beginning.

The other day as I walked with a basket of laundry through the room, Tom gathered me in his arms just as the first strains of "Stairway to Heaven" floated from the speakers. And when he sang "Stairway to Helen's," I was transported back in time when nothing mattered except our love.

Helen Kay Polaski

Linda's hunk alarm goes off.

Have We Met Before?

A kiss is a lovely trick designed by nature to stop speech when words become superfluous.

Ingrid Bergman

The warm and balmy weather created a perfect night in Southern California for the first outdoor party of summer.

Wearing my best white summer dress to show off my newly acquired tan, I applied my makeup perfectly. My honey blond hair shined like a new penny and bounced in a pageboy when I walked. I looked like a "hottie," and I knew it.

Busy talking to my friends, I saw some movement out of the corner of my eye. A tall, handsome guy had just walked into the backyard and took my breath away. Older than all the other high school boys at the party, he stood out as a college man. I remembered one of the girls, Anne, said she had invited her older brother.

"Wanna dance?" I heard his deep voice beside me.

"Sure," I replied, certain he could hear my heart beating in my chest.

We danced cheek to cheek under the moonlight and talked about everything under the sun.

Elvis crooned "Love Me Tender," and we danced every dance together. I had never experienced the feelings I felt for this person; it was as if I had known him my entire life.

With my brain in a whirl and my knees weakened, I walked into the house for a drink of water.

"Just met the guy I'm gonna marry," I called out to the girls standing around the kitchen. They all looked at me in stunned silence.

I breezed back out the door, not wanting to be out of his arms for a second.

The night finally ended, and I gave him my phone number, hoping he'd call.

There was just one little snafu. I was leaving on vacation the next morning—two weeks at Lake Tahoe. My parents couldn't understand my reluctance to go—I had convinced myself that Paul would forget me by the time I returned. He probably knew lots of college girls. I was just a high school junior.

I moped around during my entire vacation and read romance novels by the pool. My parents urged me to go to a dance at the local teen center. I stubbornly said no. I had found my guy, and I didn't want to meet anyone else.

Every day I sent him postcards—not the small size, the giant 5 x 7 variety. I wanted to make sure he didn't forget me.

When I returned, I waited for the phone to ring—nothing. So I took things into my own hands and planned a backyard party.

All my friends came, and I held my breath, waiting to see if Paul would show.

Finally, I heard it—his voice.

"Hi there! I guess you've been in Tahoe by the looks of my mailbox."

"Yeah, you didn't forget me while I was gone, did you?" I asked, grinning sheepishly.

"How could I? I have enough postcards to paper my room. You are one crazy chick. I'm going to call you 'nutscake.'"

"I'll allow that if you dance with me," I stated boldly.

"I like a woman who knows what she wants," he said, taking my hand and placing it on his shoulder. "You know, it's funny, all the time you were gone I felt like I knew you from somewhere. Have we met before?" he asked as we swayed together, cheek to cheek.

"Never," I replied.

So, he felt it, too, that feeling of connectedness.

"Let's go for a ride in my car so we can be alone and talk."

"I can't leave my own party!" I cried.

"Sure you can. Look around; no one will notice. Everyone is too busy having a good time."

He was right, everyone was having a ball, dancing, and talking, and pairing off for the evening.

"Okay, but just for a little while."

We sneaked out the side gate, and then it happened. He turned abruptly, taking me in his arms. I remember that night like it was yesterday. I can still close my eyes and smell his cologne and feel his soft lips on mine. I tingled down to my toes.

"Let's go," he said in a husky voice.

We drove down to the beach, laughing, talking—Paul with his arm around me and me snuggled up beside him.

Forty years later, we're still together, snuggling and laughing. He still calls me his "nutscake." I still remember that kiss, the romance of that night, and all the years that followed. The tall college man and the girl with the shiny blond hair have passed the years convinced they've known each other since forever.

Sallie A. Rodman

Soul Mates

You, my love, hold my heart
And touch my soul,
Ignite my passion
And make me whole.
You comfort me, strengthen me
And dry my tears.
You inspire me
And soothe away my fears.
The sunshine of your laughter
Brightens each day.
Sharing joy and sorrow with you
Means more than I can say.
Knowing you care eases my strife.
You give me the happiness,
I have longed for all my life.

Karen E. Rigley

The Magic Rock

As the sun started to go down, my daughter, Savannah, snuggled up against me to fight off the autumn chill. "Tell me a story, Mom! Please!" she begged. Unlike the countless times she pleaded with me to read her worn fairy tale books at home, I did not need persuasion this time to share my fairy tale-like story. This buried treasure had lived in my heart for twenty years and awaited discovery.

Pulling her closer, I whispered in her ear, knowing that this would thrill her little soul. Not only does this darling daughter of mine love fairy tales, but also finds great delight in sharing secrets. Savannah listened attentively as I shared the reason why we make our seasonal trips to this special spot.

One fall day, Terry (my prince and Savannah's dad) drove me back to Murray State for my last year of college. Although this would be my last year of college, it would also be the first time in six years that I would not see Terry on a daily basis. After graduating in the spring, Terry had accepted a position at a regional accounting firm—but in a different region from where I was! Since the firm was six hours away from campus, I knew his visits could not be frequent. Spoiled by the six years of being his almost constant companion, I knew that I would cry if I tried to speak, so I kept silent the entire two hours of our drive to campus.

As he pulled off the main highway onto the winding road that took us to our special spot, Terry broke the silence by telling me that we needed to talk. As we climbed the steep bluff, my heart raced not from the exercise, but from the wonderful anticipation of being alone with him. Countless times we had enjoyed talking and relaxing in the sun on this particular rock that overlooked the lake. Not only did we always enjoy watching the boats, but also found great delight in looking at each other.

When we finally reached the rock, I cried.

Terry just held me. When he thought I had finished, he reached into his pocket and got out some coins. Exactly one nickel and three pennies. Terry explained that the eight cents stood for the eight months before our wedding date. I wanted us to bury these coins with the promise of uncovering them when we were to wed. As we buried our treasure, the golden oak leaves began to fall—much like my tears.

Over those eight months, Terry's phone calls, letters, and occasional campus visits helped make our separation a little less tearful. However, when I really missed him, my heart warmed with the thought of that golden day when we buried our treasure. Our treasure, covered with dirt, was also blanketed by snow.

The winter melted into spring and the months of waiting were also disappearing. When graduation day arrived, many of my friends said that I glowed. The reason behind my rosy cheeks was not only from my happiness of obtaining my degree, but also from the anticipation of the treasure hunt that followed graduation exercises.

As we climbed the steep bluff this time, my heart once

again raced! Oh, how I prayed those coins stayed where we had placed them! After a few unsuccessful digs, we finally located our treasure. As the sun warmed the copper pennies, I reminded myself of that golden autumn day when we had shared our secret. We returned to do what we had promised. After sharing a few kisses that day in the sun, we took our treasure with us. I felt like a princess as I glanced one more time at the castle. Walking hand in hand to our car, we laughed and teased each other about sharing this story someday with our children.

This magical day turned into night as we went shopping for our wedding bands. After the jeweler showed us many rings, we knew that for us there was only one choice. We chose simple golden bands. Golden like the falling leaves when we made our promise, and like the sun that kissed our lips when we found our buried treasure.

As I finished my story, Savannah's eyes twinkled as she said, "Then I guess this rock is magic! Right, Mom?" Looking at her father holding her little brother, I agreed. "Yes, Savannah, this rock is magic! It is where dreams were made, and now they have come true."

Every fall when returning to Murray State's homecoming, we visit what Savannah has named the Magic Rock. After twenty years, I am happy to say that I am still under the spell. Each time I climb the steep bluff, my heart races not from the exercise, but from my overwhelming emotions. Overwhelmed by precious memories from the past as well as memories in the making.

Stephanie Ray Brown

Stop the Car!

Love is the greatest refreshment in life.

Pablo Picasso

My heart thundered in my chest as a man ran out in front of our car.

"Stop the car! Stop the car!" he shouted, holding his hands out.

Two more men raced up and pounded on our windows. "Stop the car," they screamed in unison. We stopped.

A face appeared in the window. "Put your window down!" the man insisted.

I sat motionless and mute as my husband Joe reached down to open his window.

It was the night of our thirteenth (yes, lucky thirteen) anniversary. Joe and I had just dined at an Italian restaurant in celebration. We spent the entire evening absorbed in each others' company, oblivious to those around us. We held hands and talked.

Dean Martin's voice filled the air with "That's Amore" as our waitress brought out fresh garlic bread and salad. I remember glancing up for an instant and noticing three couples seated at the table beside us, but I was soon reabsorbed into the trance of our evening.

Then Joe got on his knees and pulled out a card from under his chair and handed it to me. The card was full of beautiful words, and I smiled and kissed him. Joe reached down and got his calendar, and we planned a family camping trip to take place later that summer. We looked forward to taking our three children camping on our favorite island in Michigan. Suddenly, all was silent.

"Oh, no—everyone's gone!" I said glancing at the empty tables around us.

"We'd better go," Joe said.

We paid our bill and walked hand in hand to our car.

It was when we were driving out of the parking lot that the three men stopped our car and insisted we put our window down. My heart raced as Joe cracked his window a couple of inches. The men looked into our car.

"We have to know," one said breathlessly.

"Know what?" my puzzled husband asked.

"Did she say yes?"

"What?"

"Did she say yes?"

Our fear turned to laughter as we recognized the faces as those belonging to the men at the table next to ours. The couples were sure they had witnessed a marriage proposal at our table.

"Yes, she did." Joe responded with a smile. "Thirteen years ago!"

Sandra R. Bishop

More Chicken Soup?

Many of the stories you have read in this book were submitted by readers like you who had read earlier Chicken Soup for the Soul books. We publish many Chicken Soup for the Soul books every year. We invite you to contribute a story to one of these future volumes.

Stories may be up to 1,200 words and must uplift or inspire. You may submit an original piece, something you have read, or your favorite quotation on your refrigerator door.

To obtain a copy of our submission guidelines and a listing of upcoming Chicken Soup for the Soul books, please write, fax, or visit our website.

Please submit your submissions through our website:

www.chickensoup.com

or via mail to:

Chicken Soup for the Soul
P.O. Box 30880, Santa Barbara, CA 93130
fax: 805-563-2945

Supporting Others

In the spirit of supporting others, the publisher and coauthors of *Chicken Soup for the Soul Love Stories* will donate a portion of the proceeds from the sale of each copy to the **Horses and the Handicapped of South Florida.**

The Horses and the Handicapped of South Florida is a peaceful place in the middle of the hustle and bustle of city life where people with special needs can share a sense of belonging with a horse and a dedicated group of volunteers. Located in a 700-acre park in Coconut Creek, Florida, they cater to the special needs community by offering equine-assisted therapies for children and adults with physical, cognitive, and emotional difficulties.

Horses are partnered with students in a program that sets specific goals, including right-left discrimination, balance, and socialization. Under the supervision of physical therapists and certified NARHA (North American Riding for the Handicapped Association) instructors, a team of volunteers work with their students toward the student's individual therapy goals. The riding facilities have been designed with the program's participants in mind, seeking to provide a safe and recognizable setting that fosters a greater level of comfort and familiarity for challenged riders and their families.

Horses and the Handicapped of South Florida, Inc., is a non-profit organization founded in 1982 and has been approved as a Premiere Accredited Center by NARHA, meeting standards that put this program in the top 25 percent of all the 726 accredited programs across North America.

Horses and the Handicapped of South Florida is a place where people come to heal, to learn, and to make friends that last a lifetime.

Horses and the Handicapped of South Florida, Inc.
Mandy DeBord, Executive Director
P.O. Box 273542
Boca Raton, FL 33427-3542
www.HandHMagic.org
HandH@HandHMagic.org
Phone: (954) 974-2007
Fax: (954) 974-6119

Who Is Jack Canfield?

Jack Canfield is the cocreator and editor of the *Chicken Soup for the Soul* series, which *Time* magazine has called "the publishing phenomenon of the decade." The series now more than 140 titles with over 100 million copies in print in forty-seven languages. Jack is also the coauthor of eight other bestselling books including *The Success Principles*™ : *How to Get from Where You Are to Where You Want to Be, Dare to Win, The Aladdin Factor, You've Got to Read This Book,* and *The Power of Focus: How to Hit Your Business, Personal and Financial Targets with Absolute Certainty.*

Jack has recently developed a telephone coaching program and an online coaching program based on his most recent book *The Success Principles.* He also offers a seven-day *Breakthrough to Success* seminar every summer, which attracts 400 people from about fifteen countries around the world.

Jack is the CEO of Chicken Soup for the Soul Enterprises and the Canfield Training Group in Santa Barbara, California, and founder of the Foundation for Self-Esteem in Culver City, California. He has conducted intensive personal and professional development seminars on the principles of success for more than a million people in twenty-nine countries around the world. Jack is a dynamic keynote speaker, and he has spoken to hundreds of thousands of others at more than 1,000 corporations, universities, professional conferences and conventions, and has been seen by millions more on national television shows such as *Oprah, Montel, The Today Show, Larry King Live, Fox and Friends, Inside Edition, Hard Copy,* CNN's *Talk Back Live, 20/20, Eye to Eye,* the *NBC Nightly News,* and the *CBS Evening News.* Jack was also a featured teacher on the hit movie *The Secret.*

Jack is the recipient of many awards and honors, including three honorary doctorates and a Guinness World Records Certificate for having seven books from the *Chicken Soup for the Soul* series appearing on the *New York Times* bestseller list on May 24, 1998.

To write to Jack or for inquiries about Jack as a speaker, his coaching programs, trainings, or seminars, use the following contact information:

Jack Canfield
The Canfield Companies
P.O. Box 30880 • Santa Barbara, CA 93130
phone: 805-563-2935 • fax: 805-563-2945
E-mail: info4jack@jackcanfield.com
www.jackcanfield.com

Who Is Mark Victor Hansen?

In the area of human potential, no one is more respected than Mark Victor Hansen. For more than thirty years, Mark has focused solely on helping people from all walks of life reshape their personal vision of what's possible. His powerful messages of possibility, opportunity, and action have created powerful change in thousands of organizations and millions of individuals worldwide.

He is a sought-after keynote speaker, bestselling author, and marketing maven. Mark's credentials include a lifetime of entrepreneurial success and an extensive academic background. He is a prolific writer with many bestselling books, such as *The One Minute Millionaire, Cracking the Millionaire Code, How to Make the Rest of Your Life the Best of Your Life, The Power of Focus, The Aladdin Factor,* and *Dare to Win,* in addition to the Chicken Soup for the Soul series. Mark has had a profound influence on many people through his library of audios, videos, and articles in the areas of big thinking, sales achievement, wealth building, publishing success, and personal and professional development.

Mark is the founder of the *MEGA Seminar Series. MEGA Book Marketing University* and *Building Your MEGA Speaking Empire* are annual conferences where Mark coaches and teaches new and aspiring authors, speakers, and experts on building lucrative publishing and speaking careers. Other MEGA events include *MEGA Info-Marketing* and *My MEGA Life.*

He has appeared on *Oprah,* CNN, and *The Today Show.* He has been quoted in *Time, U.S. News & World Report, USA Today, New York Times,* and *Entrepreneur.* In countless radio interviews, he has assured our planet's people that "you can easily create the life you deserve."

As a philanthropist and humanitarian, Mark works tirelessly for organizations such as Habitat for Humanity, American Red Cross, March of Dimes, Childhelp USA, and many others. He is the recipient of numerous awards that honor his entrepreneurial spirit, philanthropic heart, and business acumen. He is a lifetime member of the Horatio Alger Association of Distinguished Americans, an organization that honored Mark with the prestigious Horatio Alger Award for his extraordinary life achievements.

Mark Victor Hansen is an enthusiastic crusader of what's possible and is driven to make the world a better place.

Mark Victor Hansen & Associates, Inc.
P.O. Box 7665 • Newport Beach, CA 92658
phone: 949-764-2640 • fax: 949-722-6912
website: www.markvictorhansen.com

Who Is Peter Vegso?

Peter Vegso arrived in South Florida from Canada and founded the publishing company Health Communications, Inc., in 1976. HCI's first *New York Times* bestseller, *Adult Children of Alcoholics* (Woititz), appeared on the list in 1985 and has been followed by dozens more self-help and inspirational titles, including *Healing the Shame That Binds You* (Bradshaw), *A Child Called It* and *The Lost Boy* (Pelzer), and many titles in the Chicken Soup for the Soul series. Recognized twice by *Publishers Weekly* as the #1 Self-Help Publisher, HCI is guided in its publishing program by its mission statement, "Making a difference in the lives of our readers and the people they come in contact with."

Peter's other business interests include a professional publishing and conference company that provides training, licensing, and certification for members of the mental health community, a custom design and architectural elements manufacturer, and real estate development.

Peter enjoys his 140-acre farm in Ocala, Florida, where he continues to expand his successful thoroughbred breeding and training facility. Daily operations are handled by the hardest-working manager in the world, Chuck Patton, who shares Peter's intention to not only win the Kentucky Derby but also the Triple Crown before their spirits leave this planet.

Peter Vegso
Health Communications, Inc.
3201 SW 15th Street
Deerfield Beach, FL 33442
phone: 954-360-0909 • fax: 954-360-0034
website: www.hcibooks.com

Contributors

Nancy C. Anderson (www.NancyCAnderson.com) is a popular speaker and the author of "Avoiding the Greener Grass Syndrome: How to Grow Affair Proof Hedges Around Your Marriage." Nancy lives in Orange County, California.

Aaron Bacall has a graduate degrees in organic chemistry as well as in educational administration and supervision from New York University. He has been a pharmaceutical research chemist, college department coordinator, instructor in college, and cartoonist. He has sold his cartoons to most national publications and has had several books of his cartoons published. Three of his cartoons are featured in the permanent collection at the Harvard Business School's Baker Library. He continues to create and sell his cartoons and is writing a book. He can be reached at ABACALL@MSN.COM

Suzanne Baginskie has been employed as a legal assistant at a law firm for more then twenty-five years. Recently, she taught a creative writing class at the local college. She currently is penning her first romantic suspense novel and lives on the west coast of Florida with her husband, Al.

Mary Ann Bennett-Olson was born in the quaint little town of St. Thomas, Ontario, Canada, and was raised by her doting grandparents, who showed her that the world is truly remarkable and that the course of someone's life can change in an instant. Meeting her husband was one of her life's greatest gifts.

Sandra R. Bishop is a graduate of Purdue University School of Nursing and enjoys capturing humanity and good humor in her writing and photography. She continues to honeymoon with her husband of twenty-nine years in Indiana. They have four beautiful children, two amazing sons-in-law, and one adorable grandson. Sandra can be reached at frostymom21@hotmail.com.

Arthur Bowler, a US/Swiss citizen and graduate of Harvard Divinity School, writes, speaks, and ministers in both English and German. His writing has appeared in several bestselling anthologies and in bestselling books in Switzerland. Look for his book *A Prayer and a Swear* or visit Arthur at www.arthurbowler.ch.

Stephanie Ray Brown of Henderson, Kentucky, has been married to her Webster County High School and Murray State University sweetheart, Terry, for twenty years. When their life gets a little crazy raising their two children, Savannah and Cameron, Stephanie often finds herself longing for those lazy days when she spent countless hours just holding Terry's hand on their Magic Rock, where and when it truly did seem like time stood still. Stephanie loves to hear that a story so near and dear to her heart has touched another. Stephanie can be reached at savvysdad@aol.com.

Carol Bryant met her husband, Phil, while working on a traveling nurse assignment in Hawaii. They have now been married for twenty-three years and have two daughters, Cassie and Lauren. They have turned their travel experiences into the foundation for their travel business. Carol is now a full-time travel agent, part-time nurse, wife, mother, and mediocre tennis player.

Julia Burnett is a watercolor artist. Her mother was her inspiration, teaching her early on how to see and appreciate beauty in all things and encouraging her to capture it on paper. An avid gardner, her gardens and the wildlife within are often the subjects for her paintings. Julia can be reached at arthummer@aol.com.

April Smith Carpenter received her Bachelor of Arts from Lambuth University and her Masters of Religion from Memphis Theological Seminary. She is a devoted mom to Brooks and Grace, and she adores her husband, David, of seven years. She enjoys writing, football, traveling, and teaching aerobics. April can be reached at carpenteraprilsmith@yahoo.com.

Joan Clayton is a retired teacher. She is the author of eight books and is a religion columnist for her local newspaper. Joan has been in *Who's Who Among America's Teachers* three times. She and her husband will soon celebrate their fifty-ninth anniversary. Joan can be reached at joan@yucca.net.

Helen Colella is a freelance writer from Colorado. Her work includes educational materials (geography and history workbooks), articles, and stories for adults and children, contributions to nine Chicken Soup for the Soul editions, and numerous parenting magazines. She currently operates AssistWrite, a business offering writing and consultation services to independent publishers. Helen can be reached at helencolella@comcast.net.

Tracy Kirk Crump is a freelance writer living in Mississippi. She has been married to her first love, Stan, for thirty-one years. They have two grown sons, Brian and Jeremy. Tracy can be reached at tracygeneral@gmail.com.

Clinical instructor **Ray Duarte**, RN, a grantee for his research (April 1993), is referenced in the *New England Journal of Medicine* (March 1990). With thirty abstracts and nine manuscripts published, his focus has pivoted from technical to creative writing, which you can find in *Seniority* magazine. Visit Ray at www.geocities.com/dna_93105/.

Terri Duncan is a closet writer who is ready to come out of the closet. She has been published in several Chicken Soup titles as well as other publications. She is a veteran educator, the proud mother of two teenagers, and also very much in love with her husband.

Janet Perez Eckles is an inspirational national speaker, freelance writer, and contributor to seven books. She authored *Trials of Today, Treasures for Tomorrow: Overcoming Adversities in Life*. Janet and her husband live in Florida, and she imparts insights, inspiration, and messages to uplift the soul. Visit Janet at www.janetperezeckles.com.

Amanda English is seventeen years old and is currently a senior at Smyrna High School in Smyrna, Delaware. She enjoys horseback riding, softball, painting, and hiking. Amanda is active in student government, Student Leadership Academy, 4-H, Business Professionals of America, and is the current president of her chapter of the National Honor Society.

Peggy Frezon is a freelance writer from New York. She loves spending time with her wonderful husband, Mike, her kids, Kate and Andy, and dog, Kelly. Her stories appear in *Guideposts, Sweet 16, Positive Thinking, Angels on Earth, Teaching Tolerance, Chicken Soup for the Soul, Soul Matters,* and other publications. Visit Peggy at http://peggyfrezon.googlepages.com.

At age ninety-three, **Manny Gold** is still happily married to his wife, Sylvia. They are as deeply in love now as they were when they first met sixty-one years ago. They have a son and a daughter, two grandsons, and three great-granddaughters.

R. Goulet is a High School graduate with no previous writing experince. He retired from the Rock Island Illinois Fire Department. Robert lives in Matlacha, Florida and now works part time doing condominium maintenance. He flies back to Illinois every other weekend to visit his grandchildren and to enjoy the beautiful yard he and Estelle loved so much.

A retired nurse practitioner, **Nancy Harless** divides her time between her home in Wever, Iowa, and traveling around the world—always on a shoe-string, usually off the well-traveled road—with her husband, Norm. Her first book, *Womankind: Connection and Wisdom Around the World* will be released October 2007.

Emily Sue Harvey, author and speaker, writes to make a difference. She is convinced that love and compassion make the world go round. Her insights have converged into upbeat fiction and nonfiction stories and novels that ring of triumph in the face of adversity. Peter Miller's New York agency represents Emily Sue. Her mainstream novel *Unto These Hills*, set on a southern Mill Hill, now makes the publishing house rounds. Emily Sue currently serves as president of the Southeastern Writers Association. Emily Sue can be reached at EmilySue1@aol.com.

Jonny Hawkins' cartoons have appeared in over 350 publications, over 100 books and in his own cartoon-a-day calendars over the last twenty years. His latest book, *The Awesome Book of Healthy Humor,* is available everywhere. He lives in Sherwood, MI with his wife, Carissa, and their three children—Nate, Zach, and Kara—to whom he delightfully dedicates these cartoons. He can be reached at jonnyhawkins2nz@yahoo.com.

Peter Hesse, a WWII vet and graduate of R.I. School of Design, is a graphic designer/art director, cartoonist, and watercolor painter. Since 1970, he and his wife, Liz, have lived in Denver, Colorado. They have four children and five grandchildren. You can contact Peter via his website at www.cartoons byhesse.com.

Allie Hill is a high school student in Ontario, Canada. She's a vegetarian and animal rights activist who loves writing, reading, and playing football with her two dogs and brothers. She plans to write fiction novels after furthering her education, and thanks Mrs. Lunn for always inspiring and encouraging her.

Donna L. Hull is a Tucson-based freelance writer. She shares a love of travel with her husband, Alan. From Bali's beaches to hidden canyons in the American West, she writes about adventures that encourage readers to get up off the couch and go. Donna can be reached at dlhullwriter@yahoo.com.

Cindy Hval's work has appeared in *Chicken Soup for the Mother and Son Soul, Chicken Soup for the New Mom's Soul,* and *Cup of Comfort Devotional for Mothers.* She's a correspondent for the *Spokesman Review* newspaper in Spokane, Washington, where she and her husband are raising their four sons. Cindy can be reached at dchval@juno.com.

Paul James was born and raised in Detroit, Michigan. After high school, he joined the Navy to see the world. Today James works for his favorite chocolate factory; however, his passion is to write stories people will enjoy. Paul's wife and girls are his chief editors and resource for ideas.

Mother of seven and grandmother of seven is how **Eva Juliuson** is usually described. She shares God's love through writing, teaching, and working with kids. She sends out regular short e-mail prayers to help jump-start others into a deeper prayer life with God. To receive them, e-mail her at evajuliuson@hotmail.com.

Paul Karrer has been published in Chicken Soup books, the *San Francisco Chronicle,* and numerous magazines. He reads his short stories most months on NPR station KUSP in Santa Cruz, California. He is a sixth-grade teacher, union negotiator, and a scourge to his teenage daughter. He lives in Monterey, California, and can be reached at pkarrer123@yahoo.com.

Alison Kay Kennedy lives in California and will be starting ninth grade next year. She wrote the poem "A Gift for Heaven" in sixth grade. Alison wants to be a journalist when she grows up, writes poems and stories, and loves to play with her two dogs in her spare time.

Betty King is the author of four books: *It Takes Two Mountains to Make a Valley, But—It Was in the Valleys I Grew, The Fragrance of Life,* and *Safe and Secure in the Palm of His Hand.* She is also a newspaper columnist and speaker. Visit Betty at www.bettyking.net, or she can be reached at baking2@charter.net.

Joyce Laird is a freelance writer based in southern California. Her fiction and "slice of life" features have been published in magazines including *"Woman's World," "Grit,"* and *"Vibrant Life."* She is also a contributor to *Chicken Soup for the Dog Lover's Soul.*

Trina Lambert is a Colorado-based writer who lives with her husband, daughter, and son. Most of her pots and pans, along with with her marriage, are approaching the twenty-year mark—and she wouldn't have it any other way. She and her husband plan to grow obsolete together. Visit Trina at www.trinalambert.com.

Michelle Lawson is a stay-at-home mom to three great kids. She resides in Vancouver, British Columbia. She enjoys reading, traveling, sewing, crafts, and writing. This is her second Chicken Soup story and she plans to continue writing more stories in the future. She would also like to dedicate this story to her husband, who is always her inspiration.

Jaye Lewis is an award-winning inspirational writer and frequent contributing author to Chicken Soup for the Soul. She lives with her family in the beautiful Appalachian Mountains of Virginia, which Jaye insists is the most romantic-place on Earth. Visit Jaye at www.entertainingangels.org, or she can be reached at jayelewis@comcast.net.

Heather Cook Lindsay lives in Bangor, Maine. She is currently writing a memoir about her unusual life, including the years she spent living in an oxygen tent and her ongoing battle with chronic illness. She graduated from Mount Holyoke College and Harvard University. Heather can be reached at hclindsay@aol.com.

Barbara LoMonaco received her Bachelor of Science degree from the University of Southern California and has elementary school teaching credentials. Barbara has worked for Chicken Soup for the Soul Enterprises since February 1998, as their story acquisitions manager and customer service representative. She is a coauthor of *Chicken Soup for the Mother and Son Soul.* Barbara can be reached at blomonaco@chickensoupforthesoul.com.

Charles Markman has been in the art business since high school. He operates a graphic design studio in Oak Park, Illinois, and has been a freelance cartoonist for many years. Now residing in south Florida he continues to produce graphic design, cartoons, and "fine art" watercolor paintings. Charles can be reached by email at cngmarkman@aol.com.

David McAmis grew up in the United States but now lives and works in Sydney, Australia. He is the author of over a dozen computer books and is working on his first novel. Visit David at www.davidmcamis.com.

Erin McCarty is a freelance writer in Erie, Pennsylvania, and the author of *The Land That Gives and Takes Away: Reflections on Little Pine Valley.* She can be found online at www.epinions.com/user-bilbopooh.

Ken McKowen is an award-winning travel author and *Chicken Soup for the Soul* coauthor (*Chicken Soup for the Fisherman's Soul* and *Chicken Soup for the Soul Celebrating Brothers and Sisters*). When he's not creating new titles for Chicken Soup and other publishers, he spends his time woodworking and cycling. Visit Ken at www.PublishingSyndicate.com.

Sharon Melnicer is a writer, artist, and teacher in Winnipeg, Manitoba, Canada. She frequently broadcasts the stories she has penned on CBC radio. A retired high school English teacher, she continues to teach Creative and Life Story Writing to adults, and is a recognized artist who shows and sells throughout North America.

Jacki Michels lives in Soldotna, Alaska. She is a wife to Ken, a mother, a stepmother, and a five-time Granny Award winner. She writes a regular humor column for the Kenai Peninsula Clarion and is working diligently to finish her first book.

Marie-Therese Miller is the author of the books *Hunting and Herding Dogs, Helping Dogs, Search and Rescue Dogs, Police Dogs,* and *Distinguished Dogs* (Chelsea House, 2007). Her story "Panic" was published in *Chicken Soup for* *the Preteen Soul 2.* She lives with her husband and their five children in New York. Marie-Therese can be reached at thisisthelife@hvc.rr.com.

Sandra Nevarez teaches third grade in Lakewood, California. As a former co-director of the CSULB Writing Project and a recipient of the prestigious CATE 2007 Classroom Excellence Award, Sandra is passionate about teaching writing to students and project fellows. She plans to write children's books. Sandra can be reached at artnevarez@aol.com.

Mark Parisi's "Off the Mark" comic, syndicated since 1987, is distributed by United Media. Mark's humor also graces greeting cards, T-shirts, calendars, magazines, newsletters, and books. Lynn is his wife and business partner. Their daughter, Jen, contributes with inspiration, as do three cats. Visit Mark at offthemark.com.

Kathleen Partak has been writing a weekly e-mail column, the "Monday Motivator," for the past eight years. Kathleen has done several short-term columns on telephony, today's technology, and mortgages. She is the proud wife of an army soldier and mother of three-year-old Mason. She also has several children's books and a motivational book in the works. Kathleen can be reached at Kdpartak@yahoo.com.

Saralee Perel is an award-winning writer, chosen in the National Society of Newspaper Columnists' competition. She's a *Family Circle* magazine contributor and a nationally syndicated columnist. Her novel *Raw Nerves* received the BookSense honor. Saralee can be reached at sperel@saraleeperel.com.

Stephanie Piro lives in New Hampshire (not too far from the beach!) with her husband, daughter, and three cats. She is one of King Features' team of women cartoonists, "Six Chix" (she is the Saturday chick!). Her single panel, "Fair Game," appears in newspapers and on her website: www.stephaniepiro.com. Her new book *"My Cat Loves Me Naked"* is available at bookstores everywhere. She also designs gift items for her company Strip T's.

Helen Kay Polaski is an author and editor. Her most recent projects included editing the anthologies *Christmas Memories, Stories to Warm the Heart and Renew the Spirit, A Cup of Comfort for Weddings,* and *Classic Christmas: True Stories of Holiday Cheer and Goodwill.* Helen can be reached at hkpolaski@yahoo.com.

Becky Povich lives with her husband, Ron, near St. Louis, Missouri. She enjoys writing, reading, photography, and creating custom greeting cards. This is her second submission to be accepted by Chicken Soup for the Soul. You may contact her at WriterGal53@aol.com.

Karen Elizabeth Rigley is a multi-award-winning author, poet, and designer who lives in the heart of the Rockies. She is an internationally published author of fiction, nonfiction, and poetry. She is also known for her unique designs and her poetry art.

Sallie A. Rodman is an award-winning writer whose stories have appeared in numerous Chicken Soup anthologies, magazines, and the *Orange County Register.* She lives with her husband in Los Alamitos, California, and still believes that love makes the world go around. Sallie can be reached at sa.rodman@verizon.net.

Robert D. Russell has been a nurse for thrity-seven years. In that time he has seen the human spirit laid bare by the unforgiving scrutiny of modern medicine. In the direst of circumstances he has been inspired by the courage of ordinary people. This is what keeps Robert writing.

Harriet May Savitz is the award-winning author of twenty-four books, including *Run, Don't Walk*, an *ABC Afterschool Special* produced by Henry Winkler. Her new novel *Sidney! Sidney! Sidney!* and reissued books by AuthorsGuild/ iUniverse can be found at www.iUniverse.com and Harriet's Web site, www.harrietmaysavitz.com. She can also be reached at hmaysavitz@aol.com, or Essay Books at www.authorhouse.com.

JP Shaw lives in Abbotsford, British Columbia, with her husband and two boys. She is currently pursuing a career as a romance novelist. JP enjoys swimming, bike riding, scrapbooking, and web design. Visit JP at jpshaw.bcinfo.com, or she can be reached at jp-shaw@hotmail.com.

Dayle Allen Shockley is an award-winning writer whose work has appeared in dozens of publications. She is the author of three books and a contributing author to many other works, including the Chicken Soup series. Dayle can be reached at dayle@dayleshockley.com.

Sarah Smiley is the author of "Shore Duty," a syndicated newspaper column, and the memoir *Going Overboard* (Penguin/NAL, 2005). Her liferights were recently optioned by Kelsey Grammer's company to be made into a half-hour sitcom. Visit Sarah at www.SarahSmiley.com.

Patricia Smith is the recipient of the Excellence in Writing Award (National League of American Pen Women) and the 2006 scriptwriting Telly for *Invaders of the National Parks,* a documentary on invasive species (National Parks Service). Her story "Can't Help Falling in Love" appeared in *Chicken Soup for the Dog Lover's Soul.*

Joyce Stark has recently retired from local government and has just completed her first book about the travels she and her husband have taken in the United States. Apart from planning their next travels, she is working on a book to teach very young children another language. Joyce can be reached at joric.stark@virgin.net.

Carol Duncan Sweet is a semi-retired grant writer and owner of Write Here, which offers creative and business writing workshops. She also teaches English as a Second Language in companies to nonnative English speakingemployees. She and Bill enjoy traveling and going to concerts. Carol can be reached at sweetwriter@gmail.com.

Sabrina Ann Taylor is a wife and mother of two beautiful daughters, Mikayla and Shyla. She works as a waitress and restaurant manager. She is currently working on her poetry projects as well as a children's book. You may contact her at mommy_bri@hotmail.com.

Arlene Uslander is the author of twelve nonfiction books, primarily in the field of child development, parenting, and humor. She has won several media awards for excellence in journalism. Uslander, now retired from full-time teaching, spends her time writing; editing; traveling with her husband, Ira; enjoying their grandchildren, Eric, Ryan, and Carly; and doing some substitute teaching—just to stay in touch with what's on kids' minds, and in their hearts, today.

Samantha Waltz is a freelance writer in Portland, Oregon. Her essays can currently be seen in the Chicken Soup for the Soul series, Cup of Comfort series, and a number of other anthologies. She has also published adult nonfiction and juvenile fiction under the names Samantha Ducloux and Samellyn Wood.

Stefanie Wass lives in Hudson, Ohio, with her husband and two daughters. Her writing has appeared in *Chicken Soup for the New Mom's Soul, Chicken Soup for the Beach Lover's Soul,* and newspapers nationwide. Stefanie is a member of the International Women's Writing Guild. Stefanie can be reached at swass@adelphia.net.

Joyce Jody Wilcox works as an Executive Assistant/Graphics Specialist. She enjoys scrapbooking and teaching it to others. The love story of her parents continues to nurture her and serves as the foundation for the wonderful love story she and her husband, Ken, will leave for their own children. Joyce can be reached at wwilcox@hvc.rr.com.

Ferida Wolff is a contributor to several Chicken Soup books. She writes books for children and adults, including the picture book *Is a Worry Worrying You?* and the essay book *The Adventures of Swamp Woman: Menopause Essays on the Edge.* Visit Ferida at www.feridawolff.com.

Thousands of **Bob Zahn**'s cartoons have been published in all the leading publications. He has more than one thousand greeting cards to his credit, as well as several humor books. Bob can be reached via email at zahntoons@aol.com or visit his website at www.zahntoons.com.

A Gift from Heaven. Reprinted by permisison of Alison Kay Kennedy and Helene Kennedy. © 2006 Alison Kay Kennedy.

The Beauty of a Dull Glow. Reprinted by permission of Patrina Sue Lambert. © 1999 Patrina Sue Lambert.

Love Is Easy; Married Is Hard. Reprinted by permission of Sharon Melnicer. © 2006 Sharon Melnicer.

When the Right One Comes Along. Reprinted by permission of Patricia Ann Smith. © 2006 Patricia Ann Smith.

Fireworks. Reprinted by permission of Allie Hill. © 2006 Allie Hill.

My Love Story. Reprinted by permission of Helen Colella. © 2006 Helen Colella.

A Babe in Boyland. Reprinted by permission of Nancy C. Anderson. © 2005 Nancy C. Anderson.

Love at Sixty Is Different. Reprinted by permission of Carol Duncan Sweet. © 2007 Carol Duncan Sweet.

Finding My Husband Again. Reprinted by permission of Saralee Perel. © 2007 Saralee Perel.

Watching from a Doorway. Rerpinted by permission of Robert Russell. © 2006 Robert Russell.

Romance. Reprinted by permission of Samantha Waltz. © 2007 Samantha Waltz.

Marriage with a Firm Foundation. Reprinted by permission of Betty Ann King. © 2006 Betty Ann King.

Love Endures, After All These Years. Reprinted by permission of Dayle Allen Shockley. © 2003 Dayle Allen Shockley.

She Had His Heart. Reprinted by permission of JP Shaw. © 2007 JP Shaw.

His Trail of Love Notes. Reprinted by permission of Sandra Mercado Nevarez. © 2008 Sandra Mercado Nevarez.

A Space of Her Own. Reprinted by permission of Nancy Leigh Harless. © 2004 Nancy Leigh Harless.

A Love Story About a Ring. Reprinted by permission of Saralee Perel. © 2000 Saralee Perel.

Presents of Mine. Reprinted by permission of Marie-Therese Miller. © 2004 Marie-Therese Miller.

Piano Love. Reprinted by permission of Donna L. Hull. © 2003 Donna L. Hull.

When the Heart Speaks. Reprinted by permission of Julia Burnett. © 2007 Julia Burnett.

The Last Dance. Reprinted by permission of Joyce Laird. © 2005 Joyce Laird.